"Court Reports from Vanessa Nelson which make you feel like you are right there, with me, fighting for medical marijuana." -- Ed Rosenthal, May 2007

U.S. vs. Ed Rosenthal 2.0
The re-trial of the Ganja Guru

Ø

Vanessa Nelson

Published by Medical Marijuana of America
www.MedicalMarijuanaofAmerica.com

ISBN 978-0-6151-6084-9

In Memory of Virginia Resner (1946-2007)
    who teaches me still
        and has my admiration always

CONTENTS

Introduction

E dward "Ed" Rosenthal was well known long before his trial made international news. His books on marijuana cultivation, many of which have sold over a million copies, had already earned him undisputed status as an expert in his field. This reputation was further cemented by his wildly popular "Ask Ed" column, which has run in magazines for over two decades. With all this under his belt, fame was undeniably solid for Rosenthal by the time feds came banging on the door of his Oakland home on February 12th, 2002...but Ed Rosenthal was about to get even more famous.

The high-publicity raid netted marijuana starter plants Rosenthal had been growing in order to supply local medical marijuana dispensaries, an activity for which he had been deputized by the City of Oakland. It also landed Rosenthal in jail for a short time, but bail secured his quick release and allowed him to stay out of custody leading up to his January 2003 trial in federal district court.

A key issue in the pre-trial hearings was whether the jury would be allowed to hear evidence that Rosenthal's plants had been grown for medical purposes. Although medical marijuana has been legal in California since 1996, its continued prohibition under federal law ultimately prevented Rosenthal from mounting a medical defense during trial.

The jury came back with a guilty verdict for the defendant, but soon afterwards the case developed a unique twist – upon learning the truth about the medical nature of the grow, the jurors were outraged and publicly recanted their verdict. Although Rosenthal was already convicted, Judge Charles Breyer took the juror revolt into account during sentencing and handed down a jail term of just one day, time served.

Rosenthal retained his status as a convicted felon until April 2006, when the 9th Circuit Court of Appeals reversed his conviction and remanded the case to U.S. District Court. Determined to reaffirm Rosenthal's status as a felon, the U.S. Attorney promptly filed a superseding indictment that not only brought back marijuana cultivation charges but also added tax evasion and money laundering counts.

But the government's new case hit a snag in early 2007, when the defense filed a motion claiming vindictive prosecution. A key component of this motion was a transcript of Assistant U.S. Attorney George Bevan, Jr., saying that the financial charges had been added to the indictment as a result of his displeasure with comments Rosenthal had made to the press. Working for the defense, attorney Joseph Elford of Americans for Safe Access successfully argued that the new charges were brought as a vindictive punishment for Rosenthal's exercise of his right to free speech. Granting the motion, Judge Breyer dismissed the tax evasion and money laundering counts. Only the marijuana charges remained, but the government stuck to those charges doggedly and persisted in taking the case to trial.

Given that Bevan already declared he would not seek additional penalties on the remaining charges, this was an unusual prosecution. All the U.S. Attorney stood to gain was a reaffirmed conviction for Rosenthal, but the government pushed towards trial nonetheless, ignoring Judge Breyer's repeated warnings that the proceedings would be a waste of resources.

It was a situation that perplexed the public, frustrated the judge, and challenged the defense. But by May 2007, the stage had been set and the re-trial officially began. The venue and most of the characters were the same as before, and the world watched closely to see if the outcome would be different this time around.

Photo 1 - Ed Rosenthal and his defense team, left to right, Omar Figueroa, Ed Rosenthal, Shari Greenberger, Robert Amparán by Vanessa Nelson

U.S. vs. Ed Rosenthal 2.0

Monday, May 14th, 2007
Jury Selection

During six hours of intense questioning, a group of 90 men and women was gradually whittled down to form the jury for the re-trial of Ed Rosenthal.

As is typical of such proceedings, a negotiating process between the defense and prosecution weeded out the candidates who displayed the strongest views on the topics presented. That part was expected.

But what was unusual was the vociferous passion demonstrated by this group of prospective jurors, many of whom transformed the interviews into a soapbox for vocalizing their support of medical marijuana.

Beginning at 8:30am, each potential juror filed into the courtroom carrying a paper clearly marked with a two-digit number that would be the sole means of identification for the first round of questioning.

For this round, Judge Breyer read off questions and the jurors answered by silently raising their numbered cards for display. The judge then recorded which parties had answered for each question. It was a tedious recitation of numbers that inspired him to humorously comment, "I feel like I'm at a kind of a church bingo, without the payoff."

But with hundreds of thousands of dollars poured into this case, and the felony status of a prominent community member hanging in the balance, the stakes seemed a bit too high for bingo.

And, true to their nature, the proceedings sobered up very quickly. As soon the questioning began, in fact, it became clear that some very contentious issues were afoot.

The first subject was the federal prohibition on marijuana, but the judge embarked on a bit of a preamble before finally posing his starting question. "Marijuana is the subject of some controversy in this country," Judge Breyer told the larval jurors. "It is also the subject of some laws in this country. Maybe that is what causes the controversy. I don't know."

After that flirtation with philosophy trailed off, Judge Breyer got down to business. "Under federal law, and this *is* federal court, it is illegal to grow and possess marijuana.

Photo 2 - Ed Rosenthal
by Vanessa Nelson

How many of you hold views that are contrary to this law?"

An impressive 54 cards went up. A statement had been made.

After recording the responses, the judge turned to his second question...and his second preamble. "In this case, there may be evidence that the defendant grew for medical purposes," Judge Breyer said carefully before hammering down a legal understanding. "Federal law, *not* California law, is applicable to this case. Federal law does not allow you to consider the medical aspects of marijuana."

So introduced, the judge presented the second question, "Do you hold views on the medical aspects of marijuana?"

Over 80 cards were thrust into the air, some with demonstrable gusto. On a visual scan, it seemed as though it could be unanimous. Certainly Judge Breyer thought so. "This may very well be everybody," he commented as he looked out over his bench at the sea of numbered cards. On official count, there were only a scattered handful of dissenters.

And, though it demonstrated the power and salience of the issue, this question was precisely the one that dismayed the defense.

Rosenthal's lawyers had fought vigorously to prevent prospective jurors from being asked about their beliefs regarding medical marijuana. If the defense attorneys feared that such questioning would lead to the purposeful dismissal of medical marijuana supporters, their concerns were well grounded.

The questioning created a confusing situation for some of the potential jurors – they were told by the judge that a medical defense would not apply to the case and that this defense would not be presented, so why were they being questioned about medical marijuana at all?

During their individual interviews, many of the prospective jurors voiced frustration over this conflict. "I can't convict someone in federal court on a crime that was legal under state law," one woman said with a tone of distress.

Other prospective jurors voiced the conflict as outrage, as did one man who said pointedly, "I don't think the federal government has any business in the state of California. And I think this case is all about sour grapes."

Several gave concise lectures about the resources wasted in this investigation, and also in the prosecution of marijuana offenses in general.

A swarm of others attacked marijuana prohibition as being "flawed," described the trial as a case of "unfortunate scapegoating," and accused the prosecutors of caring more about politics than justice.

A retired nurse used her interview time to state her desire for uniform regulation of the medical cannabis industry. "I strongly believe in the use of medical marijuana," she said. "I think it should be legalized and controlled as other drugs are."

More compelling were the short testimonials given by various health care workers who had nursed terminally ill patients.

A physician described the experience she had with medical marijuana treatment while working at San Francisco General Hospital. "It was very effective," she said with emphasis. "And sometimes it was the only treatment that was effective."

"I could not serve on this jury," another retired nurse said emphatically. "I have worked extremely hard to get Proposition 215 passed. I have also given and procured marijuana for many of my oncology patients. I did it gladly, and I would do so again."

Rounding off the perspectives were those decidedly against marijuana, be it medical or otherwise. Though in the minority, these potential jurors were as well-spoken as their counterparts on the other side of the issue.

Two cited moral objections to all drug use, including the use of marijuana.   Another two briefly described the negative experiences of witnessing substance abuse by close family members. The remaining few in this group talked about the protective role they play as parents, and stressed the importance of keeping their children away from drugs of any kind.

One woman, now retired from data security work at Pacific Bell, spoke in great detail of the detrimental effects that marijuana has had on her family. After informing the courtroom that her niece's husband is currently in jail for possession, she described the lengthy detox and recovery experience of her nephew. "It took us 12 years to get him off of marijuana and back in school, but he's successful now," she said in dramatic tones, before concluding that she fully agrees with federal drug laws.

All in all, the proceedings had begun to sound less like jury selection and more like the public comment segment of a spirited city council meeting.

Whatever the occasion, one thing was clear: when it came to the subject of medical marijuana, this was an extraordinarily vocal group of citizens. Even bright and early on a Monday morning, nearly all of them were thoughtful, intelligent, and articulate in their views.

Expectedly, many of these jurors-in-waiting had such strong views that they reported they would be unable to decide the verdict impartially. And, expectedly, these jurors were all dismissed.

In the end, there remained only the most soft-spoken of the lot. The survivors were four men and eight women who had either declared no opinions or who had convincingly demonstrated that their views could be set aside while considering the case. Plucked from amongst their more outspoken peers, these jurors were positioned to decide the guilt or innocence of Ed Rosenthal. Already sworn in on their oaths, they were ready to sit with wide eyes and open ears for opening statements the next morning.

U.S. vs. Ed Rosenthal 2.0

Tuesday, May 15th, 2007
Opening Statements

Day 1 of Ed Rosenthal's re-trial was one hell of a roller-coaster ride.

Over the course of seven hours, Judge Breyer's courtroom underwent a fascinating, multi-stage metamorphosis of mood. An atmosphere of excitement quickly deteriorated into bizarrely antagonistic dullness, creating a tension that finally erupted in heated admonishment and threats.

And all of this occurred on a day that began with displays of the utmost in cheerfulness and cordiality. The jurors filed in at 8:30am, fresh out of the chill of a windy San Francisco morning, and things got rolling fast. They barely had a chance to warm up their new seats for the first time before they were hit with a barrage of information about people, places, dates, times, events and actions.

It was open season for opening statements. This was the time for the attorneys on both sides to outline what the evidence of the case would show, and also their chance to make a first impression on the newly-formed jury.

The government, represented once again by George Bevan, started out with the requisite gratitude and thanked the jurors for the sacrifices they were making. But that gratitude came with a reminder of the responsibilities of their civic duty.

"You took an oath," Bevan said to the jurors soberly. "You raised your right hand and promised you would fairly judge the facts, and you promised you would apply the law as Judge Breyer instructs you to apply it."

The federal prosecutor then told the jury that he would present evidence of a large marijuana grow operation, and of plots and conspiracies involved with that operation. They would learn about a criminal cash economy, about fallen alliances, and about an undercover buy involving hundreds of plants and hundreds of thousands of dollars.

According to Bevan, the evidence would show that Rosenthal was involved with marijuana grows at three locations: a warehouse on Mandela Parkway in Oakland, a property across the street from his home on E. 22nd Street in Oakland, and at the Harm Reduction Center on 6th Street in San Francisco. More specifically, Bevan gave a detailed outline of what the evidence would show in relation to each of the charges against Rosenthal.

- For Count 1, the government would show that Ed Rosenthal, Kenneth Hayes, and Richard Watts conspired to use the Harm Reduction Center to grow and distribute marijuana.
- For Count 2, the government would show that Ed Rosenthal and others used the Harm Reduction Center to knowingly and intentionally grow and distribute marijuana.
- For Count 3, the government would show that Ed Rosenthal and others conspired to manufacture, possess with the intent to distribute, and use two locations (on Mandela Parkway and on E. 22nd Street) to manufacture and distribute marijuana.
- For Count 4, the government would show that Ed Rosenthal knowingly and intentionally possessed marijuana for distribution and used the Mandela Parkway property for that purpose.

- For Count 5, the government would show that Ed Rosenthal utilized the Mandela Parkway facility for manufacturing and distributing marijuana.

Bevan concluded his opening statements with a plea to the jurors to remain open-minded while hearing the case. He compared the process to assembling a puzzle, saying that it goes together piece-by-piece, and that you don't get the whole picture until all those pieces have been properly placed. However clichéd, it was a quaint analogy.

What Bevan lacked in flourish, attorney Shari Greenberger

Photo 3 - Shari Greenberger
by Vanessa Nelson

more than compensated for during her opening statements for the defense. She began with a warm hello to the jury, addressing them as "fellow citizens of *California*" with great emphasis. Greetings done, Greenberger promptly sunk her teeth into a passionate argument that the case against her client was an attempt at government censorship.

Over the past 40 years, the defense attorney said, Rosenthal has been a successful author and researcher, as well as a scientist of international acclaim. His knowledge and reputation afforded him the opportunity to testify as an expert witness in state and federal courts. "His testimony in defense of medical cannabis did not endear him to the federal government," said Greenberger.

Bevan objected to this statement, and the opening argument paused as Judge Breyer considered what had been said. After a few moments he over-ruled the objection, deciding that Rosenthal's expertise in growing marijuana was relevant to the charges. He even went so far as to say that the presentation of such evidence might be more beneficial to the prosecution than to the defense. "One could argue, Mr. Bevan, that this is evidence *you* could introduce," the judge mused.

Greenberger continued by showcasing her client's work, flourishing a bottle of the natural herbal pesticide "Zero Tolerance" that Rosenthal developed through the application of his skills in botany and horticulture. She also brought out a large box of books Rosenthal had authored and published, displaying them to the jury with gusto. Even when she fumbled and dropped an armload of them on the floor, the effect was still dramatic – there was a sense of abundant, overflowing information.

"The government is attempting to suppress his ideas," Greenberger said about the alleged censorship of her client, "and that is why we are here."

Bevan also objected to these statements, gaining more favor with the judge this time. According to Breyer, the jury should be asked to decide the case based on the evidence presented, not based on a consideration of the government's motivation for bringing the charges. "That's a decision the government is entitled to make," Breyer explained to the jurors. "It's not a decision that you, the jury, or me, the judge, should pass judgment on."

Greenberger aborted her accusations regarding the government's motivations, but went on to lean heavily on her claims about the underlying self-interests of the government's witnesses.

With vivid, evocative language, she described the character and the possible motivations of several of the witnesses who would be testifying against Rosenthal during the trial. Greenberger told the jury that the evidence would show that these individuals were testifying in exchange for plea deals that granted them probation instead of decades in prison. She detailed the crimes of the government witnesses, which included everything from marijuana cultivation to spousal abuse and ticket scalping.

"It's important to evaluate the credibility of the witnesses, and inquire on their motive for being here," Greenberger urged the jurors. "They are convicted felons, liars, drug addicts, and thieves."

Neither are the law enforcement witnesses necessarily more credible, she suggested, reminding the jury that these officers get paid to give their testimony. Similarly, the officers often engage in practices of deception, Greenberger said, and this was precisely what happened in the undercover buy that Bevan mentioned in his opening statements.

"Agent Chris Fay used false pretenses to get into a dispensary to purchase marijuana that was intended for patients," Greenberger alleged. Her statement was an attempt to cast a shadow of doubt on the officer's trustworthiness, while simultaneously slipping in a subtle reference to medical marijuana.

It was a characterization that the judge later felt compelled to clarify to the jury. Responding to the defense's statements about the dishonesty of undercover officers, Judge Breyer explained that law enforcement officers are not precluded from stealth and deception, and that they are entitled to use a wide range of deceptive techniques in order to carry out their work. He told the jury that they should be aware of this fact while hearing evidence of the undercover operation involved in this case.

Having now exhausted her sensationalistic portrayals of the shady doings of government witnesses, Greenberger held up the defendant as a contrast to all this criminality. She told the jury that Rosenthal had no criminal history other than what was being brought against him in this case. She added that the same could be said of Rosenthal's wife, Jane Klein. "Consider these differences with the other witnesses," Greenberger suggested to the jury. "Contrast [Klein and Rosenthal's] unblemished records with the witnesses the government is going to bring."

Ms. Greenberger's black-and-white presentation had all the moral ambiguity of an old Western flick. She lowered the government witnesses into a seething cesspool of vice and selfishness, only to raise her client up onto a pedestal of heroic stature.

It was a bold and powerful approach. It was also a risky one. Drama has its draw, most certainly, but there's danger in letting the fireworks steal the show.

Later on in the afternoon, out of the presence of the jury, Judge Breyer expressed his impression of Greenberger's argument. "I don't know based on your opening statements if you're contesting the facts," the judge said to the defense counsel. "I know you question the credibility of the witnesses, but that's all I know from your opening."

Greenberger's absolutist presentation may have gone a bit far in another area as well. Skeptical of the claim that Rosenthal's criminal history was completely blank, Bevan used a court recess to dig up the pre-sentence report on the defendant.

Once the jury had been excused for the day, the prosecutor described the results of his research to the judge. According to Bevan, Rosenthal has a 1971 arrest for marijuana, a 1995 arrest for possession of marijuana for sale, and an incident in Atlanta, Georgia, involving interference with enforcement of the law.

This is not a perfect record, according to Bevan, and he declared that representing it as such misled the jury. The judge assured Bevan that he would look more closely at the wording in the transcripts regarding this portion of the opening statements, but also offered the prosecutor some basic advice. "If Ms. Greenberger said something you think the evidence contradicts, then submit the evidence," he said simply.

Government Witness John Pickette

For its first witness in the case, the government called DEA Special Agent John Pickette to the stand to testify in front of the jury.

Pickette answered questions about surveillance he conducted in November 2001 at the Mandela Parkway property, a location where Rosenthal was accused of cultivating marijuana.

The agent described the presence of a few vehicles, including a white BMW registered to Douglas Church, a brown Mercury registered to Gary Schwartz, a silver BMW registered to Etienne Fontan, and a silver Mercury registered to Edward Rosenthal. At one point, according to Pickette, Rosenthal exited carrying a plastic grocery bag of unknown content. Accompanied by another subject, Rosenthal left the Mandela Parkway facility and drove away in the silver Mercury.

Although Pickette lost surveillance with the car twice while following the subjects, he ultimately trailed the car to the Harm Reduction Center at 52 6th Street in San Francisco. There, as Pickette described it, Rosenthal and his companion entered with the grocery bag. The pair exited the location after 20-30 minutes, but did not leave with the grocery bag. They drove back to Mandela Parkway, where Rosenthal's companion got out of the car and entered the driver's side of the silver BMW. Both Rosenthal and the other subject then left the area in separate cars immediately.

Pickette next answered questions about the purchase of marijuana plants from the Harm Reduction Center, which Bevan occasionally abbreviated as the "Harm Center." The agent who went undercover for this operation was Christopher Fay, and Pickette's role was just handling the evidence. He described taking custody of the 405 marijuana plants that were purchased, then counting them, sorting them, and entering them into evidence.

Upon the conclusion of this statement, Bevan produced a box that he referred to as Exhibit 74a and placed it on the witness stand. After looking down at the box, Pickette confirmed that he was the one who sealed that box of evidence. Following Bevan's direction, the agent then opened the box with scissors and described its contents: two DEA evidence bags containing marijuana, and also three telephone books, between the pages of which all 405 plants had been dried in a manner similar to pressing flowers.

Appearing satisfied with the questioning of his witness, Bevan gave up the floor to lead defense attorney Robert Amparán for the first cross-examination. This redirect had none of Bevan's brevity, however, and it ended up coming across as an exercise in stalling.

During the morning recess, Amparán had described to a colleague his strategy for the cross-examination: to drag it out as long as possible in order to make the other government witnesses wait longer than they might otherwise be required.

Photo 4 - Robert Amparán
by Vanessa Nelson

It was the beginning of a tense antagonism that would thin out the courtroom spectators and infuriate the judge.

After spending several minutes listening to the defense attorney lead Pickette around a circular questioning pattern about his job title, Judge Breyer called the subject "time-consuming" and ordered Amparán to move on. The defense attorney obliged, next asking Pickette to list and spell the names of each person who worked in his office. Amparán slowly recorded the information on paper as the agent named off his co-workers. Often, the defense attorney failed to hear Pickette's recitation and asked him to repeat for clarity. Time dragged by.

Bevan was stoic, but the spectators looked confused. Some rolled their eyes and sighed. Others giggled, giddy from enduring the excruciating dullness. Most, however, decided they had heard enough, and exited the courtroom.

When Judge Breyer interrupted again, his tone belied a waning patience. "You have already been admonished on this," he warned the defense attorney.

The warning did not prevent Amparán from continuing with his tactics, this time asking Pickette to list other investigatory government agencies. Amparán plodded along, recording these names at the easel until the judge made it clear that he found this topic irrelevant as well.

The storm was brewing, but it didn't erupt until the issue of the plant stakes was raised. On this matter, the defense attorney had the witness identify several dozen plant labels that had been taken as evidence during the undercover operation at the Harm Reduction Center. Some of the stakes were printed with the word "Medifarm" and some were not.

Upon questioning, Pickette stated a belief that the labels indicated the names of different strains of marijuana, rather than indicating the name of the producer of the marijuana. Amparán attempted to ask why different strains would be important to someone working at a dispensary, but his line of questioning failed to go anywhere significant before Bevan's inevitable objection. Since Judge Breyer had issued various rulings that a medical defense was inapplicable, Amparán was skating on very thin ice in front of an already-exasperated judge.

The defense attorney didn't appear concerned about the growing tension, and went on pleasantly to his next tactic.

Amparán asked Pickette how many stakes were without the "Medifarm" marking, but the witness didn't know. Upon the suggestion that the witness count the stakes in order to answer the question accurately, Judge Breyer interjected. He would have no counting of the stakes, but Amparán attempted to argue for it nonetheless.

That was it.

A breaking point had come.

The judge abruptly sent the jury out of the courtroom and then turned to address the defense attorney.

First, the judge asserted his power over courtroom reality. "He's *not* going to sit there and count all the stakes!" Judge Breyer declared, exasperated. "There are lots of ways to ask this question without making the witness count them!"

Then the judge launched into a quick-fire lecture. "Mr. Amparán, I have several rules," the judge continued, voice raised. "One – you are not permitted to argue with a ruling in front of the jury. Two – you are not to express a view that the court is unfair in any argument you make, in comments you make, or in body language in front of the jury. Three – attorneys cannot argue their case through questioning."

Judge Breyer's next comment on the matter conveyed a hint of the ominous. "As a general case, when lawyers start to argue with the judge, they lose," he warned the defense. The judge then explained that jurors have the sense that rulings are done fairly and will distrust a lawyer who is argumentative with a judge's rulings.

"It's to the *detriment* of your client, not the *benefit* of your client," Judge Breyer said to Amparán about his behavior in court.

Government Witness Gary Schwartz

The lengthy examination of John Pickette pushed the brief testimony of Gary Schwartz past the lunch hour. Once Schwartz was finally called to the stand, he seemed anxious but maintained his composure during Bevan's short series of inquiries. By answering these questions, the witness established himself as the owner of the brown Mercury that was present during the DEA surveillance of the Mandela Parkway facility. He also confirmed that he is the father of a young man named Evan Schwartz, who was the sole driver of the car in 2001. With these details in place, the government's examination was over in just a couple minutes.

Photo 5 - Omar Figueroa
by Vanessa Nelson

Defense attorney Omar Figueroa took up the cross-examination, but this also proved to be remarkably short. The way it appeared, Figueroa's purpose was simply to elicit mentions of medical marijuana. After Schwartz explained that his son used the car to drive to work, Figueroa asked if he knew his son was working in the medical marijuana field. Bevan objected, but Judge Breyer allowed the questioning to continue, giving Schwartz the opportunity to answer with an unequivocal 'no.' Bevan objected again to Figueroa's next question, which asked Schwartz if he *later* learned his son was involved with a medical marijuana nursery. This time, the judge sustained the objection and cut the line of questioning short. Within seconds, both sides had declared they had nothing further to inquire, and Schwartz was excused.

Government Witness William McRea

William McRea, a former hydroponics shop owner, took the stand in the mid-afternoon. He was called by the government in order to identify receipts for equipment Rosenthal had allegedly purchased. The lengthy, detailed testimony about repeated product orders was considered relevant by the judge, but it tested the endurance of a courtroom audience that had already been thinned out by tedium.

Responding to Bevan's questioning about his background, McRea started out by stating that he had earned his undergraduate degree in Agricultural Science at U.C. Davis and then obtained a graduate degree in Business Administration. He also told the court that he was the former CEO of a family agricultural business that had operated for decades before finally closing in bankruptcy in 2002. It was this business, called McCalif Growers, which had generated receipts for sales to the defendant.

Although McRea testified that he didn't personally remember meeting Rosenthal, he said that the sales receipts demonstrated that the defendant was indeed a customer of his business. At that point, Bevan began the process of having McRae read aloud the contents of four manila envelopes containing receipts that spanned over three years of sales. Time after time, McRea cited a date, an order number, a product description and a quantity.

It was droning work, with the same products making appearances over and over again. Propagation flats were a favorite, with antifungal pesticide, root cubes, and plastic humidity domes also proving popular. But it was plant labels that really interested this customer – he appeared to prefer them white, in all sizes, and in huge quantities. Their mention grew so frequent that the effect was nearly hypnotic. Judge Breyer leaned back in his chair, sighed and closed his eyes. As the monotonous testimony continued, the judge appeared pained and began rubbing the bridge of his nose.

The witness competently finished up the reading session, and then went on to answer a few more questions from the prosecutor. McRea confirmed that the shipping address for all of these orders was 1635 E. 22nd Street, a property Bevan tied to Rosenthal during opening statements. The prosecutor then had the witness examine a large poster-board containing several pictures of a grow operation. Bevan pointed at many of the items depicted in the photos, including propagation flats and humidity domes, and asked if the things in the picture were things that McRea sold at his store.

When McRea answered affirmatively, Bevan stepped it up a notch and asked the witness if the items in the pictures came from his store. "Yes, it would appear that they did," McRea said. Satisfied, the prosecutor brought his questioning to a close.

Undeterred by earlier difficulties, Amparán came forward to cross-examine the witness. The defense attorney first questioned McRea about the meetings he had with the U.S. Attorney about his testimony, and the witness admitted that the government paid his travel expenses for these trips.

On a speculative note, Amparán turned to the theory that there was a causal relationship between Rosenthal's bust in February 2002 and McCalif Growers going bankrupt in June 2002. McRea, however, denied any connection between these two events.

Amparán then pointed out that there were *colored* plant labels depicted in the pictures Bevan presented, contrasting this with the fact that the enormous quantities of labels mentioned in the sales receipts were all *white*. McRea testified that he sold only white labels, and so the colored ones shown in the photo exhibit could not have come from McCalif Growers. This detail was never mentioned during Bevan's questioning about the origins of the items shown in the pictures.

More important to Amparán, though, was whether there was foundation for McRea to testify on his knowledge of these orders. The defense attorney asked the witness if, as CEO of the company, he was personally responsible for taking customer orders. McRea answered that he was not, and that he did not personally know who made specific purchases.

McRea had already been excused from the witness stand when a last-minute objection by Amparán led to another courtroom blow up. A U.S. Marshall was dispatched to retrieve McRea before he left the building, and Judge Breyer abruptly sent the jurors to their break room.

Observers began to notice a pattern: the jury being suddenly excused was a sure sign that tempers were about to flare.

Amparán was quick to detail his objection, speaking with his trademark confidence. "He is the CEO," the attorney said of McRea. "He is not the custodian of records. He has no foundation to make these statements."

Judge Breyer began to ask if Amparán was disputing whether the records were kept in the ordinary course of business, but soon the exchange got so heated that the judge and the defense attorney began talking over each other.

"Let me finish," Judge Breyer snapped at Amparán, yelling the threat, "or you're going to be spending the night *inside!*"

The ultimatum riveted the audience. There were no soft snores or bobbing heads now, and all ears were keenly focused on the bench as the judge continued.

"If you think it's your job to object to every single piece of evidence, you'll be trying this case *twice* – once in front of *me*, and once in front of the *jurors*." Judge Breyer was still seething, but he kept a certain calm composure even when his tone bordered on hysteria. "We had this discussion at the beginning of the case. You had the chance to challenge the evidence prior to trial. Do you believe you should challenge *all* evidence, even without a good faith belief?"

Amparán answered with what could only be described as righteous indignation. "I believe it's my job to represent my client zealously, within the bounds of the law," he told the judge.

The judge, face twisted in anger, went back to his original question. "Do you believe the documents were kept in the ordinary course of business?" he demanded of Amparán.

But the defense attorney disregarded the question, answering instead, "I don't believe the foundation was there."

Amparán's refusal to answer directly sent Judge Breyer up the wall. "This is not about whether a foundation was laid," the judge said, visibly at the height of his irritation. "The question is about a good faith belief that the documents were kept in the ordinary course of business. You can answer 'yes,' you can answer 'no,' or you can answer 'I don't know.'"

Amparán said he didn't know, and tried to follow up with another statement, but the judge would hear none of it. "You don't have to say anything further," he shot at Amparán before bringing the jury back to the courtroom and putting McRea back on the witness stand.

Bevan stepped up to ask the witness the question that, by now, had become so familiar, "Was it in the regular course of business to keep these records?"

McRea gave a simple "yes" and answered a few more questions on the procedures of order-taking at McCalif Growers before he was finally excused from the stand for good.

Amparán's challenge seemed to have served little purpose but to enrage the judge even further. It could all be chalked up to a bad day, but the dynamic seemed more deeply-rooted than that. A pattern of escalating antagonism was emerging.

•

Government Witness Daniel Tuey

The final witness of the first day was Daniel Tuey, a former agent of the DEA who testified to having been involved in the raids of more than 50 indoor marijuana grows. This was the man in charge of executing the search warrant on the Mandela Parkway facility on February 12th, 2002. Not only that, but he was also the man who recorded a video walk-through of the property on that day, accompanied by his own personal narration of observations.

After Tuey identified the recording, it was admitted into evidence and then promptly played for the courtroom. The jurors watched with quizzical expressions as the recording took them through room after room containing shelves of tiny marijuana starter plants that appeared to have very recently been taken as cuttings. The mother plants, as shown on the video, were found in their own separate room. Tuey narrated on the recording the entire time, often pointing out the *obvious*, such as various pieces of growing equipment, and occasionally the more *obscure*, such as a single dried marijuana leaf found in the bathroom or a sign that read "Thank You For Pot Smoking."

While watching, the jurors appeared pensive but genuinely fascinated. They were excused for the day at the conclusion of the video, and no doubt went home with visions of clones and cuttings dancing in their heads.

Wednesday, May 16th, 2007
Government Witnesses

As the second day of the Rosenthal re-trial put a parade of government witnesses on the stand, defense attorneys pushed forward with aggressive questioning and persuasive visual presentations. Their relentless ingenuity and creative persistence precipitated a series of dramatic clashes with Judge Breyer, who described the defense's behavior as a "concerted effort to influence the jury."

But it was the prosecutor who came away looking the most troubled by the defense's techniques. In fact, by the end of the day, Bevan went on court record about his fears. With a mix of woe and frustration, the prosecutor admitted that his worst worries about this case had become a reality.

In a sharp contrast to these comments, however, the day began with Bevan in full control and questioning former DEA Special Agent Daniel Tuey on the witness stand. Responding to the inquiries, Tuey said he was involved in counting the plants seized from 1419 Mandela Parkway on February 12th, 2002. The grand total, according to Tuey, was 3163. Of this number, he testified that 2692 were clones and the rest were either mother plants or plants that were, in his words, "starting to germinate."

Bevan asked Tuey about the black garbage bags shown on the video of the search scene, which had been screened for the jury the previous day. Tuey said the bags were filled with residue, leaves and stems that were leftover from processing marijuana material. The former agent testified that the agents seized at least

27

one of those bags for evidence but left the other ones behind at the scene.

This revelation inspired the prosecutor to ask about regrets. "Reflecting back to that day," Bevan said to the witness, "should the rest of them have been taken?"

Tuey responded affirmatively.

Next, the former agent identified a cardboard box that contained items seized during the search, and confirmed the names on the evidence label and the package seals. Handing him a pair of scissors, Bevan directed Tuey to unseal the box and pull out the contents, which ultimately consisted of two bags – one labeled "clones with roots" and the other labeled "clones without roots."

Bevan wanted to know if those bags contained all the plant evidence that had been found the day of the search, and asked Tuey if thousands of plants had "reduced themselves down" to what was seen in the evidence box. Tuey said yes, and the contents of the box were admitted into evidence.

It was a space-relations concept that spoke volumes about the size of the plants seized from Mandela Parkway – thousands of them could easily fit into a standard file box. It was a revealing visual demonstration, and in stark contrast to the size of the rest of the evidence seized from the facility.

Looking at all the heavy grow equipment that Bevan had to lug across the room for admission into evidence, the jury may have wondered what all the trouble was about. Ballasts, lighting hoods, high-wattage bulbs...and all for what? A bunch of incredibly puny plants?

For all the fun of watching the dapper prosecutor drag a huge, dusty fan up to the witness stand, the situation was a perplexing one. The jury was left to balance two possible conclusions: either Rosenthal was not a drug dealer after all, or else he was an extraordinarily inefficient one. Given all the proclamations of his expertise, the latter seemed dubious. And on her cross-examination of the witness, defense attorney Shari Greenberger did wonders towards confirming the first of these conclusions.

Greenberger opened with a line of questioning on the subject of training and experience. Tuey, who was recently discharged from the DEA due to "personal reasons," had served as a narcotics agent for 11 years, and was in that capacity when he executed the search warrant at the Mandela Parkway facility on February 12th, 2002.

Greenberger was eager to establish how much the witness knew about marijuana cultivation. Tuey testified to attending a 3-day course for law enforcement officers about investigating indoor marijuana grows, and also spoke of the general drug education he received at the academy. With a degree of knowledge thus established, Greenberger set out to draw from it during her next line of questioning.

Greenberger first confirmed with the witness that no budding plants were found during the search of the Mandela Parkway location. But, Greenberger asked, aren't the flowering tops of the marijuana plants the most valuable and desirable parts of the plant? Tuey agreed, based on his knowledge and experience. And, Greenberger queried, don't most growers try to maximize their cultivation area in order to get more

Photo 6 - Shari Greenberger
by Vanessa Nelson

product? Tuey also acknowledged this statement to be true. And, finally, had the agents found any currency during their search of the Mandela Parkway property? Tuey admitted they had not.

To further illustrate her point, the defense attorney put up on the courtroom projector a layout of the Mandela Parkway facility. With agent Tuey still on the stand, Greenberger went through the layout room-by-room and questioned the witness about where plants had been found during the search. No plants had been found in 8 of the property's 11 rooms, and Greenberger crossed out each area of her diagram as it was confirmed to be plant-less. Only a very small portion of the space remained when she was done – the impression that Greenberger clearly intended to make through her demonstration. The visual exercise easily held the interest of the jurors, who watched attentively and appeared to respond to the room elimination process.

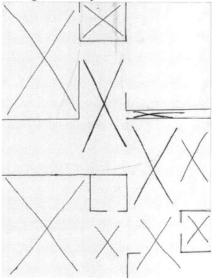

It was slightly more difficult to get the former DEA agent to state an estimate for the square footage of the building. In reaction to this, Greenberger tried repeatedly to suggest that the Mandela Parkway facility was a mere 1500 square feet. Tuey, however, only said he didn't have any

Photo 7 – Re-creation of Mandela Parkway drawing by Vanessa Nelson

idea. Though it wasn't confirmed or denied by the testimony, the 1500 number seemed to stick in the general consciousness and was likely to remain on the jurors' minds...and to serve as one more of the factors that made the Mandela Parkway grow distinctive.

The unused space, the absence of budding plants, the low square footage, and the lack of cash...all of these elements set the

Mandela Parkway facility apart from many other typical grow or sales operations. Perhaps, the jury was beginning to suspect that something atypical had been going on at 1419 Mandela Parkway. And if they had been even half as alert as they appeared to be in the courtroom, the jurors would have already received many hints that the uniqueness of this operation had something to do with science and medicine.

All in all, Greenberger's presentation seemed to be remarkably successful. With a variety of other lines of questioning, however, she was stopped short by objections from the prosecutor and, later, a harshly-delivered reprimand from the judge.

Early in her cross-examination, Greenberger took the bold step of asking Tuey if, during the time he was carrying out the search operation, he was aware that he was raiding an experimental nursery. Bevan objected, on the grounds that there had already been a court order on this testimony. The objection was sustained, and the question was struck from the record.

Greenberger presented as evidence an inspection report from the Oakland Fire Department, which evaluated the safety standards of the property at 1419 Mandela Parkway. In questioning, Tuey confirmed the document was dated before the search warrant was issued, and that this certificate had been seized during the raid on that location. The agent also agreed that the document appeared to state that the Oakland Fire Department had investigated the facility and found it to be in compliance. But when Greenberger asked if the witness knew why a commercial inspection of the facility was significant, the prosecutor objected to the relevance of the questioning. Predictably, that objection was sustained.

Greenberger then asked Tuey if he recalled seizing an item called "medical list." Bevan objected, but Judge Breyer over-ruled the objection, saying he would allow the document to be offered into evidence for limited purposes. He told the jury, "This exhibit shows a list of places that may or may not have a connection with the facility on 1419 Mandela Parkway. You are instructed that the fact that it says 'medical list' is not to be considered when arriving at a decision."

Greenberger asked where the medical list was seized from, and Tuey indicated Room 3 of the Mandela Parkway facility, but he did not recall whether it was lying on a table, filed, or hanging on the wall. Greenberger asked if Tuey saw entries on the document from the Harm Reduction Center and McCalif Growers, and Tuey said yes to both queries. Greenberger then asked about listings for other organizations, patient groups and cannabis clubs, but Tuey said he didn't know about that.

Greenberger then made a mention of Alameda County Supervisor Nate Miley. Although the judge had eliminated Miley as a witness, the defense still saw an advantage in bringing him up during the cross-examination of other witnesses.

First, Greenberger eased Tuey into a series of questions about ordinary items that had been seized from Mandela Parkway. Then she went in for the kill and asked him if the search had turned up any photographs of her client with Supervisor Miley. Bevan immediately leapt to his feet and objected. Judge Breyer was equally prompt in striking the question from the record and instructing the jury to disregard it.

Things had only just begun to heat up when Greenberger turned her attention to a seemingly innocuous evidentiary exhibit: plastic stakes that are commonly used for labeling plants. The defense counsel asked Tuey if the stakes had been seized during the search of the Mandela Parkway facility, and he said yes, but that he didn't recall which stakes were found in which rooms. Greenberger then focused on the stakes labeled "Medifarm," and asked the witness if this was related to Medicare. Tuey claimed ignorance on this matter.

Accepting that, the defense attorney posed a general question about the purpose of labeling the plants. Tuey told her that the different stakes indicated the different strains of marijuana that were being grown. Greenberger asked if some strains are used for scientific research, and Tuey said that it was his understanding that different strains are indeed used for varying purposes. The witness explained that some strains are more popular than others, such as those that have high amounts of THC.

Greenberger then shot him the key question, "Do you agree that there are specific strains that are better for treating cancer, AIDS, multiple sclerosis and other diseases?"

Bevan objected, saying there had already been a court order on this subject of testimony. Judge Breyer sustained the objection, struck the question from the record, and told the jury to disregard Greenberger's inquiry.

Trying to flesh out the witness's role in the case, Greenberger asked Tuey how long he was involved with the investigation before the execution of the search warrant. The former agent said he had been "involved in some sort of surveillance" conducted on the property a few months before the raid, but stressed that he "was not personally investigating Mr. Rosenthal."

Greenberger tried to ask about what other organizations Tuey had worked with during the investigation, about whether his department received directives from Washington D.C., and about whether the federal agents got permission from local police when doing the investigation. For every question, Bevan objected on grounds that the query was irrelevant, and, each time, Judge Breyer sustained the objection.

Undaunted by the interruptions in her line of questioning, Greenberger inquired whether Tuey had been to 1419 Mandela Parkway before the execution of the search warrant. The ex-agent said he had not. Greenberger asked, "Is it a coincidence that the same day you scheduled the raid on 1419 Mandela Parkway was the same day that Asa Hutchinson from D.C. –"

Judge Breyer hit the panic button, cutting her off halfway and quickly excusing the jury from the courtroom.

He then turned to Greenberger and asked her to repeat her question in full. She obliged, unwaveringly. "Is it a coincidence that the same day you scheduled the raid on 1419 Mandela Parkway was the same day that Asa Hutchinson from D.C. scheduled a press conference in San Francisco?"

The judge demanded to know how the question was relevant.

Greenberger simply claimed that it would show a bias on the part of the government in going after her client, but Judge Breyer wasn't convinced.

Defense attorney Omar Figueroa, who had done little vocalizing during the trial so far, tried in vain to step up and say something in support of his co-counsel. He only got out a few words before the judge instructed him to sit down. Greenberger was the one who asked the question, Judge Beyer said, so she should be the one to justify it. "It's unusual when one lawyer

Photo 8 - Omar Figueroa
by Vanessa Nelson

does the questioning and another lawyer wants to step up and say why it's relevant," he remarked.

Greenberger attempted to defend her question on the grounds that it applied to the witness's knowledge and clarified who was giving him directives. "That shows Mr. Rosenthal was targeted by the government for his beliefs," she said.

The judge told her that her theory might be used for a pre-trial motion, but that it was not relevant to a jury's consideration. "Don't ask questions in front of the jury on subjects I have already ruled irrelevant," Judge Breyer said to the defense team, echoing similar statements he made the day before. "Let me ask you this, Ms. Greenberger – if the court says something is irrelevant and not to be mentioned, do you think you should abide by the ruling?"

Greenberger responded affirmatively, but the judge quickly addressed additional violations she had made during her cross-examination of agent Tuey. Her inquiry about plant stakes, which evolved into a question regarding the use of marijuana to treat illnesses, was of particular concern to the judge.

"I understand the purpose of the marijuana," Judge Breyer told Greenberger. "I understand it was grown for the medical marijuana clubs. That's not admissible. I am instructing you not to mention the medical aspects of marijuana."

"The prosecutor opened the door," Greenberger claimed, justifying her controversial inquiry by the fact that Bevan was the one who had introduced the stakes into evidence.

"If you believe the prosecutor opened a door, then you should take it up outside the presence of the jury," Judge Breyer insisted.

The judge also insisted that the question about Supervisor Miley was improper. Originally slated as a witness for the defense, Miley was excluded from testifying by a court decision made shortly before trial. Finding Miley's proposed testimony irrelevant, Judge Breyer kept him off the witness stand...but this witness's words were making their way into the jurors' ears nonetheless.

"I don't see the basis of asking a question about a photo of the defendant with the councilman," the judge said to the defense. "I ruled that it was irrelevant, that it was prejudicial."

But the question itself was not the focus of the judge's disapproval. Interestingly enough, the majority of Judge Breyer's concerns on this matter were regarding the use of demonstrative body language by defense attorney Robert Amparán. "For the record, when Ms. Greenberger asked the question about the picture of Nate Miley, Mr. Amparán broke out in a big grin and winked at Mr. Rosenthal, clearly in the view of the jury," Judge Breyer revealed. "It was a concerted effort by the defense to influence the jury."

Amparán immediately strode forward, appalled by the judge's

Photo 9 - Robert Amparán
by Vanessa Nelson

comments. "Can I address the accusations the court has hurled at me?" he asked.

Like Greenberger's claim that the prosecutor opened the door to her questions about the medical uses of marijuana strains, Amparán's argument directed the blame for his behavior to Bevan. "I winked because of Mr. Bevan's response, not in response to Ms. Greenberger's question," Amparán told the judge, his demeanor defiant. "That the court would jump to the conclusion that there's some kind of conspiracy amongst the defense—"

Judge Breyer interrupted to correct the wording, reminding Amparán he had not *actually* alleged a conspiracy.

"Your co-counsel asked an improper question," the judge continued, speaking to Amparán. "I don't know whether you're condoning that, but the point is – you should sit there at the defense table and *not* communicate your views of the proceedings to the jury."

The defense then took issue with fact that the prosecutor had not been admonished for his reactive body language in front of jurors. Amparán suggested that it was unfair to be singled out due to a smile when the prosecutor had not been held responsible for shaking his head and frowning in the presence of the jury.

Judge Breyer, however, believed that the blame for Bevan's reactions belonged with Greenberger and Amparán. In the judge's view, the prosecutor's conduct was motivated by the defense asking inappropriate questions of the witnesses. "You're saying, 'I don't like the way Mr. Bevan is responding to my improper conduct,'" the judge said to the defense. "You might ask yourself, 'Who is responsible for that?' and the answer is – you.

"Complaining about the way Mr. Bevan reacts to your inappropriateness is a little ironic," the judge continued, shaking his head in bewildered frustration. "I hope you consider that."

Amparán was quick with his comeback. "The irony of this does not escape me," he said to the judge.

Unsuccessful in inducing a reprimand for the prosecutor on that matter, Amparán raised another complaint – that in his questioning of witnesses, Bevan had been referring to the Harm Reduction Center as the "Harm Club."

The judge said he didn't care whether the facilities in question were called medical marijuana clubs or narcotics dens. "The jury doesn't consider that," he explained. "They just have to determine whether marijuana was distributed there." Still, in the name of fairness and accuracy, Judge Breyer instructed Bevan to refer to the facility by its full and proper name.

Also at Amparán's request, the prosecutor was ordered to no longer use the term "*so-called* marijuana clubs," as he did in his opening statement.

Bevan then reached back to the opening statements on the first day of trial and complained that Greenberger showed the jury a book called "Why Marijuana Should Be Legal." But this matter inspired little reflection or debate. Judge Breyer simply turned to the defense and said, "Please don't show any of these books in front of the jury." Though it resolved quickly, the complaint put enough focus on the opening statements to refresh the judge's memory about earlier mischaracterizations made by the defense.

In Greenberger's opening statement, she had described favorable plea deals given to government witnesses and said that the deals were made by "this prosecutor." She made the same inferences regarding the entire investigation and prosecution of Rosenthal, again saying it was all because of "this prosecutor."

To Judge Breyer, it seemed that Greenberger had put all the responsibility for the actions of the federal government personally on Bevan, and that she had done so in front of the jurors during their very first day on the case.

Judge Breyer declared Greenberger's references to Bevan in her opening statements to be "inappropriate, unprofessional, and sanctionable." The judge also went on to remind the defense, "The decision to prosecute in this case is not Mr. Bevan's – it was made by the United States Attorney in the Northern District of California."

As for the prosecutor himself, he made a similar statement to an observer who engaged him during the court recess and asked about the wastefulness of the case. "My hands are tied," Bevan said to the woman, emphasizing a sense of helplessness.

On the larger perspective, the prosecutor was clearly troubled by the way the trial was progressing. He was especially dismayed at the conduct of the defense attorneys. "There are rules to abide by in this court, and there are court orders made in this case," Bevan said. In his view, the defense was cross-examining witnesses in a way that violated the rules of the court and went against decisions made by the judge.

"This is exactly what I worried about happening in this case," he lamented.

Thursday, May 17th, 2007
The Breaking Point

The first two days of Ed Rosenthal's re-trial were characterized by the defense team's attempts to push the bounds of court rulings barring testimony about medical marijuana. Day 3, however, marked the point where the defense pushed the limits to their breaking point. After attorney Omar Figueroa was accused of personally attacking a widow on the witness stand, Judge Breyer had finally had enough. It was then that he made his final warning: if the defense attorneys didn't start complying more strictly with his rulings, he would consider terminating their cross-examination.

Government Witness John Brian Padgett

The proceedings began calmly enough, with DEA Special Agent John Brian Padgett sitting on the witness stand and being questioned by the prosecutor. The agent testified that he had been in charge of executing the search warrant at 52 6th Street – San Francisco's Harm Reduction Center.

Padgett's testimony described arriving at the site at 6:05am on February 12th, 2002, at which time he knocked on the rolling metal doors and shouted, "Police!" Getting no response, he and 16 other agents forced entry, only to encounter two more glass storefront doors where they repeated the 'knock and announce' procedure. Gaining entry, the agents performed a protective sweep of the facility and found no one present. After the sweep but before the removal of evidence, Padgett shot and narrated a video of the scene. This recording was admitted as evidence, but was not screened in front of the jury.

Padgett also reported that a total of 714 plants were found at the Harm Reduction Center – 158 clones upstairs and a multi-stage grow operation downstairs, where lights and ballasts were running.

Bevan then presented a sealed cardboard box for the witness to identify, asking him to confirm the information on the evidence label, cut open the box with scissors and remove the contents. The agent complied, identifying the box as containing evidence seized during the raid at the Harm Reduction Center. But after unsealing it and peeking inside, Padgett hesitated. He looked from side to side, clearly confused. Something was wrong.

Bevan sternly repeated his order to remove the contents, but Padgett still wavered, indecisive. As the witness remained inexplicably frozen, the prosecutor became visibly anxious. Seconds passed in strange silence. Courtroom spectators craned their necks for better views, eager to see what surprise evidence was lurking in the box. Whatever it was, it seemed to have stopped the prosecution cold in its tracks.

Nervously, Bevan again instructed Padgett to dump out the contents of the box. Instead, the witness tilted the open box forward, allowing the court to see that it was full of loose plant material. Titters of laughter sprung up all over the courtroom, and with that lighthearted mood, the box and its contents were admitted into evidence.

Defense attorney Robert Amparán took the cross-examination of Padgett, beginning by putting emphasis on the fact that the agent had been with the DEA for only four years when he was put in charge of executing the warrant. Amparán asked if Padgett was responsible for picking the date for the search, but Padgett denied this suggestion. Amparán then asked if the San Francisco Police Department had been notified about the execution of the search warrant, but the witness never had a chance to answer. Bevan made an objection right away, and the judge sustained it.

Amparán then took a different approach, asking Padgett if he had found any items bearing the name Ed Rosenthal. The agent said he didn't know, since he had never reviewed the indicia from this raid, but that he didn't recall seeing the defendant's name on anything in the facility. When Amparán inquired if Rosenthal's fingerprints had been found at the scene, Padgett said they were not. Judge Breyer jumped in to ask if fingerprint evidence had been taken at all, and the agent told him that he did not believe any fingerprints were lifted during that operation.

Warming up, Amparán wanted to know whether Padgett had been aware that searches were being conducted at other locations, simultaneous with the execution of the search warrant for the Harm Reduction Center. The witness conceded that he was aware of this fact. Pressing further, Amparán asked if Drug Czar Asa Hutchinson was personally present at any of the meetings held in preparation for serving the search warrants.

The judge had spent a great deal of the morning leaning back in his chair, eyes closed in what seemed to be either physical agony or mental reflection. At moments of deep decision, he leaned forward, eyelids down and fingertips resting on his lips. At the mention of the drug czar, however, Judge Breyer perked up outwardly, eyes wide and engaged. When Bevan objected to the question, the judge was in full and alert agreement. Inquiries about Asa Hutchinson were promptly quieted, and Amparán yielded the floor to the prosecutor for re-direct.

Examining the witness again, Bevan directed Padgett's attention to a document in a folder of receipts seized during the search of the Harm Reduction Center. In it, the agent testified, was a purchase order from December 2000 that listed the name "Medifarm." From Padgett's reading, the order was for 50 clones at a price of $5 each. This interpretation appeared to satisfy the prosecutor, who had no further questions for the witness.

Amparán, on the other hand, was far from finished. During a volley of questions, the defense attorney got Padgett to admit that he couldn't tell who wrote the receipt, whether the product had ever been delivered, and that he didn't know if the folder of receipts contained any more purchase orders from Medifarm. The judge balked at the suggestion that the witness review and count all the receipts, and Bevan attempted to pacify him by stipulating that there was only one receipt with the name Medifarm.

Judge Breyer, however, was not so easily pleased. He cut off the cross-examination and sent the jury out of the room, a familiar sign that a quarrel was brewing.

Turning to Amparán, Judge Breyer first wanted to know the reason for the question about whether the drug czar was present during the raid planning meetings. Amparán explained that the basis of the question was the fact that Asa Hutchinson had been in town and had given a speech at the Commonwealth Club at the time of Rosenthal's bust. The defense believed that proving

Photo 10 - Robert Amparán
by Vanessa Nelson

the drug czar was involved in planning the raids would show that the government had targeted Rosenthal as a scapegoat.

It was far too little to satisfy the judge. "I have ruled that the motivation of the prosecution is not a matter for the jury to consider," Judge Breyer reminded the defense attorneys, frustration intensifying his words. "Did you believe the court had not made a ruling on that?"

When Amparán tried to respond that the Asa Hutchinson question was not a major inquiry, the judge asked again if he was truly ignorant of the ruling. "You spend all day long *asking* questions," Breyer said to Amparán. "Now you can *answer* one of mine."

When the defense attorney affirmed that there was indeed a court ruling on the matter, Judge Breyer quickly embarked on a summary of the situation. "That seems to be where we part ways," the judge said. "I make a ruling, then you engage in conduct that violates that ruling, and you wonder why I, one, become annoyed and, two, seem to single you out."

Sighing sharply, he continued, "I don't want to hold you in contempt. I could, but I'm not going to. I don't want to admonish you in front of the jury, but I will. I will if this conduct continues."

Changing tactics, the judge tried to demonstrate to the defense lawyers that it was in their best interest to fully comply with the court's rulings. "If a jury sees that an attorney is lawless, it redounds to the detriment of his client," he explained. "I sat in the first case with Mr. Eye, who I thought was an excellent attorney. I excluded lots of evidence he thought he should be able to present, but there was no crossover. In fact, the jury actually complained that they didn't know it was medical, that they hadn't made the connection."

It was an argument that didn't quite make sense. True, the first trial involved a defense attorney who complied more fully with the court's exclusion of evidence, but the consequences were chaos. The jurors were so confused that one of them felt compelled to seek outside advice during deliberations, and several others were so outraged upon leaning the full truth that they recanted their verdict. Given these results, it seemed odd that Judge Breyer would want a repeat performance.

Nonetheless, the final sentence of his monologue shed some light into his reasoning. "I want this case to be considered on the law and on the facts -- not on the *wisdom* of the law, but on the law as I understand it."

Government Witness David Sihota

Expectations now solidly established, the jury re-entered the courtroom and the government called its next witness, IRS Special Agent David Sihota. He had been in charge of photographing evidence during the search of Rosenthal's home on E. 22nd Street in Oakland, and Sihota identified for the prosecution several pictures he had taken of stashes found in jars and other miscellaneous containers.

Amongst these discoveries were 67 baggies of suspected marijuana, found in the glove compartment of Rosenthal's Lincoln Mercury Cougar. Bevan brought this exhibit out and took it to the witness stand, where Sihota checked the evidence tag and confirmed that this was indeed evidence seized from Rosenthal's vehicle. The prosecutor then gave the floor to defense attorney

Photo 11 - Shari Greenberger
by Vanessa Nelson

Shari Greenberger for cross-examination.

The witness described for Greenberger the details of the raid, which had been his first drug-related search operation. He reported that the 11 officers involved in the raid gathered for a preparatory meeting directly before executing the search warrant at 6am on February 12th, 2002. Armed with a gun and a camera, Sihota went in the side door of the house after the other officers made the initial entry.

The witness described seeing Rosenthal handcuffed in a chair and wearing a bathrobe. Sihota then roamed the premises, taking pictures at his own discretion and also when summoned by other officers. Perhaps he was too focused on photography to pay much attention to the layout of the house, because on the stand Sihota was unable to recall many of the details about the rooms and their non-drug contents.

Nor did the witness remember much about the car where the 67 baggies had been seized. He didn't recall if it had an alarm, or whether or not the glove compartment had been locked. When Greenberger asked if Sihota knew the bluebook value of the car, the judge jumped in and challenged the topic. "How is this relevant? We agree that it's not a luxury automobile," Judge Breyer noted. "This is a witness who went through and took photos. He's not the owner of the car, not an expert on car sales."

Seemingly inspired by the judge's reference to car ownership, Greenberger picked up on the subject and asked Sihota who drove the vehicle. The judge once again interrupted. "Wait a minute – the vehicle was moving? I thought it was parked," Judge Breyer said half-humorously.

Predictably, the judge was frustrated by the length and the topics of the cross-examination. This time, however, he was exasperated enough to end the questioning and call for the next witness. "That concludes your examination," he declared, cutting off Greenberger and excusing Sihota from the stand.

Government Witness Anita Dobberstein

Bevan next called IRS Special Agent Anita Dobberstein. The prosecutor questioned her on her previous employment as a secretary and then as a tax fraud investigative aide, and also about her 16-year history in her current job. Then examination quickly turned to Dobberstein's role in the search of Rosenthal's home on February 12th, 2002. For this operation, Dobberstein testified that she had been a "seizing agent," a job that involves collecting evidence from the officer who seized it and then handing it over to the prosecutor's office.

Her involvement established, the witness was questioned about the evidence that was seized during that search. She was shown exhibits of suspected narcotics, including vials with a "sticky, brown substance," and containers filled with a "green leafy substance." Dobberstein readily confirmed the validity of the exhibits that bore her name. As the liaison between the officer and the prosecutor, she also vouched for several exhibits, which bore the names of other agents.

Once the drug exhibits had been admitted as evidence, Bevan moved to the non-drug items seized from Rosenthal's home. He presented pre-printed labels that bore the name "Medifarm" and the classification "Romulan," as well as a handwritten stake reading "CHAMP" and "Medifarm." Then, in an envelope entitled "2 Checks To Rosenthal From Harm," were, as promised, two checks to Ed Rosenthal from the Harm Reduction Center. It was beginning to seem like a stream of excessive evidence, and by the time the prosecutor mentioned credit card bills and phone records, the judge put an end to it.

"This isn't contraband," Judge Breyer began, growing impatient again. "How does the witness authenticate that this was really the evidence seized?"

Running contrary to the defense's tendency to argue with the court rulings, Bevan was politely accommodating of the concern. The prosecutor simply offered to let the issue go, proposing that he would question other, more qualified witnesses on this evidence next week.

After Bevan bowed out, Greenberger stepped up to handle the cross-examination on Dobberstein. Unlike the more patient prosecutor, the defense attorney was not willing to drop subjects so readily and went immediately into questioning the witness about the checks. Bevan interjected to reiterate that a more qualified witness was scheduled to testify about this evidence later, but Greenberger was allowed to continue...at least for a while.

The judge had ruled that it was relevant to ask the witness about where the checks had been seized, and Greenberger did just that. Dutifully, Dobberstein answered that the checks were on a desk, in a room labeled "O" by the agents during the search. Greenberger pressed on for descriptive details, and Dobberstein testified that Check #2 was in the amount of $1400 and had the words "consulting fee" written in the memo section. Once Greenberger began asking about who had signed the checks, however, the judge indicated that she had exceeded the limited scope of questioning he had allowed.

Judge Breyer was getting anxious about the time, and the excesses of the defense's questioning tactics only increased his worries. "Cross-examination is not a vehicle for talking about things unrelated to the trial," the judge said with emphasis. "Otherwise this trial will end up taking a whole lot longer than I promised it would take."

Government Witness Catherine Rucker

Moving along more quickly, a chemist formerly employed by the DEA stepped up to take her place at the witness stand. Like other witnesses so far, Cathy Rucker was involved in an official capacity with the investigation of the defendant. Unlike the other witnesses, however, she appeared somewhat on edge, with nervous movements wriggling through a thin composure. She held her chin at a level of pride, but she wrung her hands enough to wear them out.

Drawing from experience conducting well over 500 lab tests on marijuana exhibits, and properly outfitted with a gas chromatograph, Rucker was the chemist who performed the testing on the evidence from the Rosenthal-related raids of February 12th, 2002. At first, the bulk of her testimony appeared to be rattling off lab results for each piece of drug evidence.

As expected, Rucker reported a long, unbroken series of tests that showed a positive result for marijuana. Regarding the brown, sticky substance from the vials, Rucker stated that it was a resin containing hashish and that it had tested positive for THC. Through Bevan's questioning, she defined THC as a controlled substance that is the active ingredient in marijuana.

Defense attorney Omar Figueroa began the cross-examination, and the sense of simmering anxiety immediately erupted into a boil. His first question inquired whether Rucker was still with the DEA, and when she answered in the negative, he asked if she had been fired. Figueroa's tone was likely meant to be pointed, but it somehow acquired an unfortunate and probably unintentional mocking quality.

Rucker struggled to answer. "No," she replied, her round face twisting in dismay and discomfort.

Bevan raced to her rescue, urgently requesting a private conference at the judge's bench. "I know you don't normally allow sidebars, but this is important," the prosecutor pleaded, flushed. Spectators exchanged shrugs and quizzical glances. Something unusual, and inexplicably disturbing, was going on beneath the surface. The desperation was *visible*, the tension *tactile*, and when the air was flooded with white noise during the sidebar, the sense of chaos became *audible*.

Once those sounds of static were finally switched off and all parties had settled back into their appropriate positions, the judge addressed the jury. He instructed them not to let what they heard before the break influence their judgments, since, in fact, the witness's services were not terminated by the DEA. The judge implied that it was nonetheless improper to make the inquiry.

"There is no basis for the question that was asked," he told the jurors definitively.

The defense moved on with its questioning. "What do you do now?" Figueroa asked the witness.

"I'm a homemaker," Rucker replied, conveying no small amount of embarrassment in her body language.

Surprisingly, Figueroa did not poke further at this demonstrably sore spot. Instead, he simply switched to another tactic and pursued questions about whether the government was paying for the witness's travel expenses in order to have her appear in court. When Rucker said that it had not yet been determined, Figueroa latched on to her words. "So, depending on how your testimony goes, then they'll decide to pay you or not?"

This was cut short by a frustrated judge, who demanded Figueroa abort the line of questioning and chose another. There was nothing unusual here, the judge insisted. This was all common practice. "I know of no such case where the federal government does *not* pay for a witness's travel expenses," Judge Breyer said simply.

The defense attorney then spent a great deal of time and effort requiring Rucker to answer to her experience. Did she have a PhD, or any graduate level education at all? No. Had she won any awards for her work as a chemist? None. Had she published any research for peer review or submitted any articles deemed worthy by her colleagues? Not at all. Did she have any training in botany, horticulture or taxonomy? Nope. In fact, Rucker had so little background in these fields that Figueroa chose to challenge her knowledge of the properties of Cannabis sativa. Did she know which word indicated the genus and which indicated the species? She was clueless, but clung to the repetition that marijuana is a Schedule I controlled substance under the federal Controlled Substances Act. In a cross-examination that seemed treacherous from the start, the recitation of the law became Rucker's lifeboat.

But that lifeboat quickly capsized when Figueroa asked whether the stalks of the marijuana plant were considered illegal under federal law. The embattled witness had no idea whatsoever, and she was now caught in the swift currents of logic and linguistics. Figueroa asked Rucker if she knew of anything, other than marijuana, that tested positive for THC. Her reply was no.

Then the attorney asked if THC tested positive for THC, and there was a moment of confusion before Rucker confirmed that it did. "If THC tests positive for THC, " Figueroa said with a mood of triumph, "then there's something that's not marijuana that tests positive for THC." His declaration knitted many an eyebrow together.

Semantics aside, however, the defense had some very compelling concerns about sloppiness and harmful negligence in Rucker's testing procedures. Particularly troubling was the manner with which the former DEA chemist handled the 67 baggies allegedly found in the glove compartment of Rosenthal's car. Rucker admitted that the baggies were not weighed individually, so the only measure on record is the cumulative weight – a grand total of 47.82 grams.

Such treatment appeared to fly in the face of the government's claim that the baggies were packaged for distribution. Even Rucker, on the stand, testified that the baggies were "pre-weighed for sale" yet refused to agree that each bag was equal in weight and content. Considering that the per-baggie average was well under a gram, which is usually the smallest measure of sale for marijuana, it was unclear what kinds of pre-packaged weights Rucker was imagining when she gave her testimony. Given such tiny amounts and their unequal distribution amongst the baggies, it was quite a stretch to fathom that these little parcels were part of some professional sales operation. This was not the first time the jury was forced to consider the crucial question – was Rosenthal just an extraordinarily inept drug dealer, or was he actually not a drug dealer at all?

But reflection on that question was interrupted by the witness's next admission, which started a wave of whispers throughout the courtroom. Not only had Rucker failed to *weigh* the baggies separately, she had also failed to *test* them separately. The former DEA chemist testified that she performed individual tests on the first 15 baggies, and after getting positive results for marijuana each time, she decided to combine the contents from all the rest of the baggies into a single sample for testing. Not surprisingly, the combined sample got a positive result for marijuana. To Rucker, this lab procedure was accurate and efficient.

Figueroa disagreed. He wanted to know what would happen if there was non-marijuana material in one of those baggies that was mixed into the combined sample. "Wouldn't it cause a positive test even for what was not marijuana?" Figueroa asked.

Unable to dispute the consequence of such a scenario, Rucker instead attacked the likelihood of Figueroa's hypothetical conditions. Her strategy had all the indicators of a last-ditch attempt at maintaining credibility. "Part of my test is a visual test," Rucker reminded the court right before stepping down from the stand. Given her admitted lack of horticultural knowledge about marijuana, it was doubtful her visual test had much sophistication.

For whatever it's worth, this was the final matter presented to the jurors before they were excused and relieved of their duties until Monday. Certainly the issue was fresh in their minds as they filed out of the courtroom, but how many gave it a second thought over the weekend was anybody's guess.

The door shut behind the jury, and with clockwork predictability, the judge began upbraiding the defense. It was then disclosed that the witness had been recently widowed. After her firefighter husband died a traumatic death on the job, Rucker had quit her employment and devoted her energies to coping with the loss. A reminder of this loss, as evoked through the cross-examination, was particularly difficult to handle.

Finally, the courtroom spectators had the mystery of that dramatic moment solved for them. The image of a distraught widow being badgered on the witness stand about the consequences of her husband's untimely death was particularly compelling. This evocative scene was the catalyst for an admonishment from Judge Breyer about good faith questioning during cross-examination.

"It is misconduct to ask a question of that nature without a good faith belief that the answer will be productive," the judge explained. "Mr. Figueroa seems to be youthful. I guess he doesn't know that you have to ask questions with a good faith basis."

The judge then noted that this was the 6th time so far in this case that he had witnessed improper conduct. Figueroa stood, calmly and silently, hands clasped behind his back. He offered no words of justification for his cross-examination, but his more vocal co-counsel immediately began speaking out on behalf of the defense team.

"This court continues to cast aspersions on the defense as though there's some conspiracy to cause trouble or be bad lawyers," Amparán said, indignant.

"I am beginning to understand why custodians are being insisted upon by the defense," the judge theorized. "It's not to establish a chain of evidence, but the defense has chosen to use these people as vehicles for asking questions that otherwise would not be allowed in testimony. If there is a conviction in this case, I want the appellate court to understand why there's a record of so many custodians taking up so much time of the jury."

Once again, Judge Breyer went back to the claim that the lengthy sessions of cross-examination were delaying the case. "I received a note from a juror," the judge said as he pulled out and unfolded a piece of paper. "It reads: 'I plan to leave for Colorado on June 4th. It is for the Leukemia Society. I raised $35,000 for a hike in the Rocky Mountains. I understood this case would end by June 4th.'"

Amparán refused to take the blame. "I think the comments the court has made to the jury about delays put a burden on the defense," he claimed. "We are not being delayed by the defense. We are not here because of the *defense*. We are here because of the *government*...It's the government that has 58 witnesses, not the defense."

"They have that many because of your requirement to have foundational witnesses," Judge Breyer shot back. "You insist on bringing in foundational witnesses, then you use them as vehicles."

In an unusual move, Amparán accused the judge of using worries about the welfare of others to passively communicate his own concerns. Judge Breyer was furious at this accusation. "Limit your cross-examination to the witnesses and not to the court!" he demanded.

The judge then vowed to spend the weekend reviewing the record and detailing the violations he found there. Next week, he warned, would follow a completely different procedure. "I may terminate cross-examination," he threatened right before leaving his bench.

Upon exiting the courtroom, spectators got their last surprise of the day. Sitting in the audience seats was Scott Schools, new U.S. Attorney for the Northern District of California. This was precisely the man who had made the decision to continue prosecuting Rosenthal in a second trial, in spite of the judge's hints that it would be a waste of resources.

Shaking Bevan's hand, Schools explained that he had come to give moral support to Rucker during her challenging testimony. But the savvy listener knew there was more at play than just good-hearted compassion for a sorrowful widow. Given the level of drama in the proceedings thus far, it seemed likely that Schools couldn't resist getting a glimpse of the live action in a high-profile trial he had personally ordered.

Monday, May 21st, 2007
A New Approach

The first week of the Rosenthal re-trial ended in a climax of heated emotions, frustration and threats, but it was all water under the bridge by the time Monday morning rolled around. Judge Breyer, likely fearing another contentious week, was delighted to receive some good news from the prosecutor. Over the weekend, a flurry of emails between the government and the defense had resulted in a compromise that would expedite the case. The defense agreed not to challenge the admission of approximately fifty pieces of evidence, thereby eliminating the need for many of the custodial witnesses to take the stand and testify.

After Bevan read off the long list of evidence to which the defense had stipulated, attorney Robert Amparán addressed the judge politely. "We did in fact listen very closely to what the court said Thursday afternoon," he said, his co-counsels beaming behind him. "We have listened very closely to the court's rulings and we respect the court's rulings. We are trying to conduct ourselves accordingly."

Judge Breyer was certainly not the only one who was elated by the news. When the jurors were brought in and told that the case would now be moving along more quickly, the delight was obvious. With smiles of relief and renewed enthusiasm, they settled into their seats and awaited the courtroom action.

Government Witness James Halloran

Jimmy Halloran was the first witness called in this new era of good will. The elderly gentleman walked up to the stand with poise that was unmarred by a slight limp, and in a quavering voice, gave his age as 66. With a pristine panama hat in his hand and a handkerchief neatly tucked into his suit pocket, Halloran seemed to personify an ideal of distinguished gentility. After hours of testimony, however, the façade was worn down. It was then that the jury got a glimpse of his spiteful side, as well as a hint of violent fantasy.

Under the guidance of the prosecution's questions, Halloran painted a detailed picture of his involvement with Rosenthal. According to the witness, the story stretched back well over a decade, to a time when he was trying to grow marijuana in his basement and failing miserably at it. One of his acquaintances at the time was Rosenthal's ex, who offered the perfect solution – Halloran should read the instructional books written by the Guru of Ganja himself. Impressed by the advice and the grow tips, Halloran then took steps to meet Rosenthal personally, and soon a friendship had blossomed. And, as is so often the case with entrepreneurs, the lines between friendship and conspiracy soon began to blur.

In August 1996, Halloran officially rented the property that has been the talk of trial – 1419 Mandela Parkway. The landlord was a neighbor and good friend named Leslie Wilmer, and Halloran testified that Wilmer was fully aware of the intended use of the rental property. According to Halloran, he and Rosenthal got right to work and spent thousands of dollars creating a marijuana grow operation at that location. The set-up Halloran described precisely matched the three-stage model indicated by other witnesses: a room for clones, a room for mother plants, and a room for plants that would be allowed to bud. Halloran stated that both parties agreed that the income and expenses should be split equally, and soon their operation was producing 2000 plants per cycle, in 10-day cycles. Based on his testimony, the plants were sold for cash at approximately a dozen locations throughout the San Francisco Bay Area, and the business partners then used that cash to pay their rent and electric bills.

In a moment of transparency, Halloran reflected, "We set up after 215 was passed. We thought we had permission to." It's a sentiment that resonates with the attitudes of many medical marijuana providers who were prosecuted after the passage of California's Compassionate Use Act in 1996.

Like a true prosecutor, however, Bevan had little use for such meditations, and instead drilled the witness for the names of places or people who had been supplied marijuana through this system. Halloran listed the ones he could remember, "There was CHAMP, there was a patients' program on Divisidero, there was a club – we called them clubs – down on San Pablo in Berkeley, and on Telegraph and 19th in downtown Oakland." His characterizations made no mention that these were medical marijuana dispensaries, except for a single vague reference to one patients' program. The omission seemed perfectly in line with the prosecutor's wishes, and Bevan then proceeded with extracting Halloran's account of the demise of the partnership.

The witness testified that he and Rosenthal stopped working together in early 1998, after what was described merely as a disagreement. Halloran said he then set up his own grow facility, which he supplemented with a monthly purchase of clones from the operation Rosenthal continued to run at Mandela Parkway. According to the witness, these clones were frequently labeled with a plant stake reading "Medifarm," which was the name that was being used specifically by the defendant.

Bevan then asked questions aimed at determining the maximum number of plants Halloran purchased from Rosenthal at any one time. The witness was unsure, but ultimately testified that he never bought more than 500 clones in a single purchase. The price tag was a sticking point, however, and Halloran declared that Rosenthal's price of $7 per plant was far too high, although the price factor did not dissuade him from making continued purchases.

Before concluding the direct examination, the prosecutor intended to finish milking his witness for as many potential accomplices as he could. First, Halloran identified the names Doug, Etienne and Jose as workers who helped with cultivation chores and boxed up plants at the Mandela Parkway grow site. As for delivery services, Halloran gave up the name Brian Lundeen.

The witness also testified about phone conversations in which Rosenthal said he was going to start a grow operation at the Harm Reduction Center, prompting Bevan to ask if Rosenthal had been supplying clones to Ken Hayes. Halloran was unsure about this detail, but there was no such ambiguity when it came to Debby of the San Pablo club in Berkeley. Halloran didn't recall her last name, but he testified that, without a doubt, Rosenthal was friends with Debby and he supplied her with marijuana for her club.

As the story wound to a close, Halloran revealed that he did not escape unscathed from the massive raids of February 12th, 2002. His own home and grow operation were searched at that time, and agents discovered several thousand plants and approximately $48,000 in cash. Halloran soon found himself being prosecuted in Oakland federal court on counts relating to marijuana cultivation and money laundering.

In a key turn of events, Halloran accepted a plea deal that kept him out of prison but required him to provide truthful testimony on behalf of the federal government. He had already met Bevan while testifying for the prosecution on a separate case, and Halloran used this new opportunity to build on his prior experience and become a darling of the U.S. Attorney's Office. In fact, he cooperated so well that he soon had prosecutors doing special favors for him. At one point when Halloran was applying for a real estate license, a federal prosecutor personally recommended terminating supervised release so that Halloran could obtain this license. It meant throwing a lifetime term of probation out the window, but the wish was granted nonetheless.

As his contemporaries were persecuted mercilessly on the same charges he had faced, Halloran moved on with life in the free world and a promising new career in real estate. The inequity of the situation was not lost on the defense, and Amparán hoped to address it to some extent during the cross-examination. As predicted, Halloran's loyalties were clear, and he resisted nearly all concessions that could benefit the defense.

When Amparán showed the witness a series of photographs and asked him to identify himself, Halloran couldn't have played it any dumber. "Is that me?" he said, squinting at the picture through his spectacles. "It doesn't look like me. I thought I was better looking than that."

The defense attorney gave him one more chance. "Do you recognize your grow operation?"

"I can't identify those as being mine," was the response. For a cooperative witness, Halloran was proving to be steadfastly uncooperative.

Amparán collected the photos and began nudging the witness to establish some facts verbally. "Is it your testimony that the bud part of the marijuana plant is the most profitable?"

"Not necessarily," Halloran responded airily.

Amparán tried a different route, asking, "Is it true that there's a lot of loss in plants?" When Halloran affirmed this, there was a hint of progress. The defense attorney continued, stating that all clones will not necessarily grow into thriving, budding plants.

"What is the clone success rate?" he asked the witness.

But Halloran refused to answer the question in any of its incarnations, and was equally resistant to providing a guess. "I can't estimate that," he said with a tone of finality.

The witness was similarly uncooperative about clarifying the names of the clubs that allegedly bought clones from the Mandela Parkway grow. He admitted CHAMP was an acronym, but couldn't recall what it stood for. He also couldn't remember the names of the Oakland club or the club on Divisidero, although he did concede that the word "patients" was in the name of the latter establishment. As for the club on San Pablo, Amparán cut to the chase and asked straight off if it was called the Berkeley Patients Group. "Could be," Halloran said, indistinct as ever.

Amparán was not easily discouraged. "Is there a difference in your mind between a club and a dispensary?" he queried the witness.

Halloran had barely finished saying "no" when Bevan jumped in with an objection on the grounds of relevance. Judge Breyer, however, was not so quick to put the questioning to a halt, and allowed Amparán to continue.

The defense attorney turned back to the witness, "For both facilities, do you need to have a—"

Bevan knew his cue, and raised the objection once again. The judge had heard enough of Amparán's cross-examination of prior witnesses to know where this question was going, and he had a familiar look of frustration on his face as he sustained the prosecutor's objection.

Amparán had pledged to more strictly follow court orders about excluded testimony, but he was clearly not averse to straddling the boundary lines and ruffling a few feathers in the process. If this was indeed a kinder and gentler defense, it was still as sharply focused and boldly determined as ever.

Turning to the alleged grow operation on Mandela Parkway, Amparán asked pointedly, "Isn't it fair to say that Mr. Rosenthal refused to commit to participate in this endeavor until California voters passed Proposition 215?"

An objection by Bevan was overruled at this point, freeing the witness to give his answer. "Not at all," Halloran said coolly.

Amparán then inquired if Halloran had seen Rosenthal with any construction tools, but the witness replied in the negative. "You said that the defendant never picked up a hammer, a nail or a saw, but that he participated in the construction," Amparán pressed. "If his involvement wasn't labor, what was it?"

Halloran responded that Rosenthal's contribution had been the design of the grow operation, inspiring Amparán to inquire further about the nature of the partnership. "Isn't it fair to say that in this relationship with Mr. Rosenthal, that Mr. Rosenthal was responsible for the care of the plants and you handled the business side of things?"

"I don't know where you're going with this. I can't relate at all." Halloran was beginning to look bothered. "All responsibilities were shared."

"Is it true that Mr. Rosenthal was interested in science and research and you were interested in profit?" Amparán pressed, his language becoming more provocative.

Halloran flatly denied this characterization, looking wary of the continued escalation.

Amparán asked Halloran if he had left the partnership because of his health, but the witness shook his head and said, "I walked away because it was a love-hate relationship."

Intrigued, Amparán requested details, and the witness's colorful nature shined through as he described Rosenthal. When things were going well, Halloran related, Rosenthal was a wonderful guy. But when things were bad, they were terrible, and at those times, Halloran confessed, he simply wanted to choke Rosenthal.

Amparán's eyes twinkled at those words, but he continued to inquire about the reasons behind the breakup. "Is it true that Mr. Rosenthal came home from a trip abroad to find the condition of the plants had deteriorated?"

Halloran laughed, "What are you talking about?" His laugh continued, at once nervous and disdainful. "Not true at all."

Amparán persisted, "And that he asked what had happened?"

Halloran tried to clarify, "He didn't have to *ask* – he *saw*."

The defense attorney was on a roll, "And isn't it true that you didn't respond to his inquiries?"

"Not true at all," Halloran said, swallowing. "I just said that he could see."

As he continued, Amparán imparted increasing emphasis in his tone, "And isn't it true that you didn't answer and just stared at him angrily?"

"Erroneous," the witness was abrupt.

Photo 12 - Ed Rosenthal at home
by Vanessa Nelson

"And then Mr. Rosenthal said he wanted to see the books too?" Amparán said suggestively.

"No," Halloran could barely squeeze a word between the rapid-fire sentences of Amparán's questioning.

"And then you just threw up the papers and got angry, and it was one of those times that you wanted to choke him?" The defense attorney concluded with a flourish, using Halloran's own violent fantasy against him.

"Not at all," the witness grumbled.

"You testified that after your falling out with Mr. Rosenthal, you kept coming back to purchase plants from him?" Amparán continued, appearing to ease back from the earlier onslaught.

"He was the only one who had plants," Halloran shrugged through the explanation.

"You continuously returned to Mr. Rosenthal for plants even though you thought you were paying too much and even though at times you wanted to choke him?" the defense attorney couldn't resist the sensationalist imagery, hovering near it like a moth to a flame.

"I think you're taking that out of context," Halloran said, appearing flushed for the first time in the cross-examination.

Having adequately frazzled the witness, Amparán then went in for the finish and brought up Halloran's tendency to make sales to individuals not associated with dispensaries. "Isn't it fair to say that there was a PG&E worker who came by, and you sold a pound of marijuana to this worker?" the defense attorney asked.

Halloran admitted the allegation, allowing Amparán to inquire whether he had been criminally charged for that sale. But the witness had so much immunity that he no longer paid attention to which crimes he had been charged with and which had gone undetected. "I don't know," he said plainly.

Amparán put the question another way. "Is it true that you never told Mr. Rosenthal that you sold marijuana *outside* of dispensaries?"

Halloran appeared to interpret this as an accusation that he had sold marijuana *directly in front of* dispensaries. He reacted like he'd been hit with a jolt of electricity. "What now?!" he balked.

"Did Mr. Rosenthal have any idea that you sold outside the medical community?" Amparán asked, rephrasing his question again.

"Oh…he didn't know that," Halloran said sedately.

Acutely aware of the word "medical," Bevan had a look of expectancy on his face and, no doubt, an objection right on the tip of his tongue. It would, however, remain there. Smiling, Amparán ended his cross-examination and the court moved on to its next witness.

Government Witness David Lewis

When Dave Lewis was called by the prosecution, the gaunt 43 year-old took the stand with a touch of sadness. Bevan began examining him, and his story started to form and slowly develop. Staring softly forward through much of his questioning, Lewis told a woeful tale of addiction, incarceration and perpetual loss.

Lewis testified that his lover, Vern Anderson, had lived across the street from Rosenthal and had been employed selling the Guru of Ganja's books in the early 1990s. After Anderson's death, Lewis reported that he inherited the house and began working for Rosenthal in another capacity – drying, manicuring and selling the marijuana that Rosenthal would drop off with him.

Lewis told the prosecutor that he received free marijuana in exchange for these services, which also involved the occasional buyer coming over to Lewis's house to make a purchase that had been pre-arranged by Rosenthal. In particular, Lewis recalled a woman named Debby Goldsberry buying pounds of marijuana from him in this manner. As he described it, Goldsberry would arrive with her triple-beam scale in hand and buy pounds of marijuana for $3000 each, a price set by Rosenthal.

This arrangement went on for only three months, cut off prematurely by Lewis's arrest on November 15th, 1998 during a cannabis festival at an expo hall. As Lewis related, he was arrested by park police for distributing cookies that each contained one gram of marijuana.

After being arrested, Lewis reportedly went back to his residence with the police and allowed them to search the premises. The officers turned up a sizable quantity of marijuana, which was in Lewis's possession as a result of his arrangement with Rosenthal. However, Lewis told the prosecutor that he didn't breathe a word about the marijuana really belonging to his neighbor. "I didn't want to get anyone else involved," he said, explaining his decision.

For the cookie sales and marijuana possession, Lewis ended up with a sentence of approximately three years. Although he was initially allowed to serve it on probation, his parole was violated in 2000 when he was found to be in possession of methamphetamine. Lewis went straight to jail after that violation, and a series of events followed by which he forfeited ownership of the house he had inherited from his deceased lover.

As Lewis described it, the property went into foreclosure

Photo 13 - Jane Klein
by Vanessa Nelson

during his time in jail because the tenants failed to make the mortgage payments. His neighbors became aware of this situation, according to Lewis, because a foreclosure notice was wrongly delivered to the Rosenthal residence. At this time, some legal wrangling began. Lewis already owed money to Rosenthal and his wife Jane Klein, since the couple had been putting money on Lewis's books that allowed him to make supplemental food purchases while in jail. With their friend facing the additional financial burden of delinquent mortgage payments, the couple made a proposal to Lewis – he could sell the house to them, rather than letting it get taken by the bank. It was a solution that would eliminate Lewis's debt and also leave him with a substantial amount of money from the escrow, and he quickly signed a sales agreement. Eventually, the house was sold for $250,000 and Lewis received $46,300 from the escrow.

Bevan ended his direct examination on an odd note, scrapping chronology and asking the witness once again if the cookies he was arrested for contained marijuana. For whatever reason, the prosecutor was choosing to emphasize this point and remind the jurors of this detail. Obediently, Lewis confirmed that the cookies in question did indeed contain marijuana.

Defense attorney Shari Greenberger took on the responsibility of the cross-examination, and immediately threw all her theatrical skill into portraying Lewis's drug addiction as a cautionary tale. Responding to Greenberger's inquiries, Lewis detailed his drug history. He admitted that he had been growing marijuana since he was 13, and also confessed to dabbling with cocaine. Overwhelmingly, however, his drug of choice was methamphetamine, which

Photo 14 - Shari Greenberger
by Vanessa Nelson

he snorted or smoked on a daily basis.

Greenberger then asked several questions about the negative effects of methamphetamine use, listing off a long series of adverse conditions with a horror-story tone: disrupted sleep, dental deterioration, memory loss, depression, psychosis. Then, with equal gravity, Greenberger described the social consequences of methamphetamine use: poor management of finances, impaired judgment, rage, and social withdrawal.

The defense attorney then asked the witness if he ever stole to support his habit, citing a 2003 arrest for possession of a stolen credit card. Lewis admitted to this, and also confessed to stealing books from Rosenthal in the time period between 1997 and 2002.

Greenberger also brought up a seemingly bizarre account of an arrest in 2004 that involved "possession of a crack pipe, a stolen shopping cart, and a screwdriver" and landed Lewis in a rehab facility. Judge Breyer then interrupted her questioning and suggested that she move on, to which she responded with ambiguous sincerity, "Thank you, judge – I appreciate your guidance."

As she went on to detail more casualties of Lewis's methamphetamine addiction, Greenberger paused to pay special attention to the loss of his house. Through the kind act of a dying lover, Lewis had been willed the property so that he could have a stable home. But soon his meth addiction took over his life, getting him in such dire financial straits that he eventually lost the house. Lewis was left with only the money he received from escrow, but those funds evaporated once he combined his drug addiction with a gambling spree. "I wasted it all," Lewis said remorsefully on the stand. "I was high."

By the time Greenberger had finished the sensationalist portrayal, the jurors looked overwhelmed. Whether scared straight or merely fatigued, however, it was impossible to tell.

But the defense attorney had one more element to try to prove: that Lewis was so angry about the loss of his house that he would testify against Rosenthal as a method of revenge.

Greenberger started in with a question about whether Rosenthal had been fair in the sale of the house, and Lewis began describing circumstances that put him at a disadvantage. "He didn't give me sufficient time to get the house in sellable condition and get a good price for it," Lewis claimed. He detailed damage that had been done to the house while he was in jail, including the removal of a wall and the bungled installation of a bar in the downstairs area.

"You believe Mr. Rosenthal stole your house?" Greenberger asked, carefully building the suspense.

"Essentially, yes," Lewis replied, the perennial sadness pervading him.

He noted that the house, which sat on nearly an acre of land, had views of Oakland and San Francisco's downtown skyline, and also of the Golden Gate Bridge and the Bay Bridge. In Lewis's estimation, it could have fetched a much higher selling price if a few repairs had been made.

"If you received an extra $50,000, how long would it take you to spend it on methamphetamine?" Greenberger asked in response to Lewis's complaints about the low sale price of the house.

The audience seemed taken aback by the implicit cruelty of the question, especially as contrasted with Lewis's sorrowful demeanor. Bevan objected based on speculation and Judge Breyer sustained the objection, sparing Lewis from having to offer an answer.

Greenberger then went in for the clincher, asking Lewis about hard feelings toward Rosenthal. "You've never forgiven him, have you?"

"Oh, yes. I forgive him now," Lewis said simply, gently. "That's the past."

There was a moment of quiet reflection and redemption. Not much more could be said after that, and within minutes Lewis was excused from the stand to make way for another witness.

Government Witness Leslie Wilmer

Next on the stand was Leslie Wilmer, a former bus driver who testified that he invested in rental properties in order to fund his retirement. It just so happened that one of those properties was the notorious 1419 Mandela Parkway, eventually entangling the amiable 78 year-old in one of the most famous marijuana cultivation cases ever to hit the federal courts.

In spite of his ownership of a key property, though, Wilmer had little to add to the case. Under the prosecution's questioning, he established that he rented the building to James Halloran in 1996 and then to Ed Rosenthal in 1998. According to Wilmer, rent was paid in cash and he was aware that marijuana was being grown in the building.

Wilmer testified that his increasing discomfort with the cultivation prompted him to approach Rosenthal with an ultimatum – either purchase the property or move out. Evidently, Rosenthal was eager to buy. He purchased the building at the price of $150,000 with a series of money orders, and the deal was done.

Cross-examination was remarkably merciful to Wilmer, and he essentially functioned to fill in holes from the testimony of other witnesses. He positively identified Halloran in the photograph, disproving the theory that the subject in the picture wasn't handsome enough to really be him.

Wilmer also confirmed another statement that had formerly been denied, testifying that Halloran had indeed offered him partnership in the grow operation before later pairing up with Rosenthal. Wilmer's refusal had made all the difference between the witness stand and the defense table, and his soft eyes showed some awareness of this fact as he quietly left the courtroom.

Government Witness Nathan Tyler

If Wilmer's revelations had been dull, certainly Nate Tyler's testimony was lacking a pulse.

During direct examination, this witness revealed that he was merely the electrical contractor who was hired by Rosenthal to do work at the Mandela Parkway facility. During late 2001, Tyler testified that he did several jobs at the location and billed Rosenthal for various amounts ranging between $2000 and $3500. Tyler reported that Rosenthal paid these bills in cash, but the electrician struggled to recall exactly what work he had done on the property. He said he installed outlets and new circuits, but the big mystery turned out to be an order of approximately 65 fluorescent lamps, of which he recalled installing only one 8-foot tube.

"You bought all these and didn't install them?" Bevan asked.

Tyler suggested that they might have been intended as spares and kept in storage, but the prosecutor had a different view of the situation. "By buying for Mr. Rosenthal, you got the electrician's discount," Bevan said, suggesting that Tyler may have been buying spare parts for Rosenthal at a discount by making the items look like they were part of a work order.

It was an unusual accusation that seemed to go nowhere, except towards making it appear as though Bevan was cross-examining his own witness. On that note, Amparán took over the questioning and the witness was put into the hands of the defense.

"Isn't it true that there's nothing in there indicating that these are grow lamps?" Amparán asked, referring to the invoices.

"Correct," Tyler responded.

Just to be sure, Amparán made an emphasis on this assertion. "Would grow lights be marked specially and priced differently from a regular bulb?"

"Yes, I believe so," answered Tyler.

That satisfied, the defense attorney turned to one last issue, asking the witness if he was brought to the location by the defendant in order to do repairs based on a "fix-it list" left by the Oakland Fire Department. Tyler readily confirmed this, and also agreed that he was called back to the location so that he could be present when the fire department did its final review.

Oddly enough, the prosecution did not object and the judge did not intervene. As such, Tyler's questioning was remarkably straightforward and concluded quite silently.

When the jury was excused, however, Judge Breyer once again challenged the defense to explain the relevance of testimony about the Oakland Fire Department.

"The government makes an argument that this is some closed, surreptitious drug lab," Amparán offered. "We want to show that a governmental body knew about it."

The judge was unconvinced. "The government hasn't argued that," he said flatly. "If they do, then it might be relevant."

Government Witness Thomas Thompson

The day came to a steady anti-climax with the testimony of a pest control technician who admitted to spraying the Mandela Parkway building for ants in 2001. Thomas Thompson reported the types of details that other servicemen had testified about: that Rosenthal had paid in cash and that the business was called "Medifarm."

When Bevan asked him if he remembered that this was a marijuana grow, Thompson was unsure. He didn't recall how he was informed of this fact, but suspected it had been told to him over the phone. "I knew before I sprayed that this was a marijuana growing place that was under the auspices of a government agency of some type," Thompson testified.

Under cross-examination by the defense, little of interest came to light. Thompson was unable to recall whether it was Rosenthal or someone else who was at the property during his service calls, but no one seemed terribly dismayed about his lapse of memory.

"When you arrived on site, were you asked to use food-quality products because the stuff inside was meant for human consumption?" Amparán inquired.

"I would have probably determined that myself," the pest man said stuffily. "But I don't recall."

Grasping, Amparán asked Thompson to mention four or five things that he could remember about the facility. Judge Breyer, eyes closed under the weight of the boredom, simply said, "No."

Without explanation and without argument, this ended the testimony of the pest control technician. The witness was excused, and he appeared as happy to leave the stand as the spectators were to see the day come to a close.

A Sour Note

In spite of a few uneventful objections, the day's cross-examinations were generally quick and fairly sedate. But if the defense expected a reward for their efforts to fall in line with the judge's wishes, they were sadly mistaken. Judge Breyer had something else in mind for the afternoon – the continued castration of the defense's case. Witness by witness, he whittled it away, denying the tenant of the Harm Reduction Center's former site, a current business partner of the defendant, the attorney on the purchase of Lewis's house, and several others.

Expert witness Chris Conrad was initially denied, although Judge Breyer later stated that he would allow Conrad to give testimony about whether the baggies from Rosenthal's car were possessed for sale. And, in a strangely double-edged manner, the judge decided that Jane Klein's testimony was not relevant unless Bevan introduced more financial evidence that connected her to the case.

Judge Breyer characterized the situation quite succinctly. The prosecution might try to prove that Rosenthal dealt drugs by demonstrating that he operated in a cash economy. In order to counter this claim, the defense could show income related to the publishing business, and Jane Klein's testimony would be relevant in this regard.

The prosecutor then promptly obliged, announcing a piece of evidence for which he would be providing an offer of proof. "There was an issue made on cross-examination about fancy cars," Bevan told the judge. "It suggests to the jury that Mr. Rosenthal is not a man of extravagant means. The only thing we would put in is private school tuition paid for with money orders purchased with cash, to a total of $15,000."

By its nature, that move was a risky one. Education may be costly, but it was doubtful that the jury would see it as an extravagance. On the contrary, it might have shown Rosenthal to be a man whose priorities and morals fell right in line with those of the jury. It would be difficult enough to fault a wealthy man for financing his child's education, but if the jury saw Rosenthal as anything short of affluent, he would come off looking like a hero who selflessly penny-pinched to finance a good education for his daughter.

Controversial indeed, the announcement of Bevan's proffer ignited a minor debate between judge and defense counsel.

"Paying for things with cash does not mean someone is selling pounds of marijuana," Amparán argued.

"The issue is – to what extent does he pay his living expenses in cash?" Judge Breyer explained to the defense. "People who are involved in drugs, from time to time, pay their bills in cash, for a variety of reasons."

"I don't want the jury thinking that Mr. Rosenthal is walking around with pocketfuls of cash," Amparán admitted. "That's my concern."

"It seems to me that it's a cash business, and he pays his bills by cash," the judge observed. "That is relevant in determining the charges."

Judge Breyer stood firm, and his denials conveyed a sense of his larger perspective on the law. As the judge saw it, Rosenthal's attorneys had been working aggressively and sometimes on the offensive, but at the end of the day their role was strictly as the defense. As such, the judge believed their arguments must be tailored to, and thus restricted by, the attacks that were made on them.

The denial of the defense witnesses reinforced concepts that were crucial to the judge's effort to put each side neatly in its place. With decorum restored in his courtroom, Judge Breyer tried to order into black-and-white the nuances of an amazingly colorful case.

Tuesday, May 22nd, 2007
Snitches Speak, Defense Rests

Courtroom spectators got quite a show during Day 5 of the Ed Rosenthal re-trial, at the conclusion of which the defense alarmed the judge by declaring that it would rest without calling any witnesses. This was a bold move, and a dangerous one too, but it appeared to get immediate results. Judge Breyer, ever mindful of what an appeals court might decide, was dismayed by this development. If appealed to the 9th Circuit Court, trial records might reflect that his narrow rulings on witness testimony precluded the defense from presenting its case.

Photo 15 - Robert Amparán and client Ed Rosenthal by Vanessa Nelson

It was a situation Judge Breyer was eager to prevent, and he tried to entice the defense to take a night and sleep on the decision. The judge's concessions were met with scathing and imagery-laden commentary from the defendant himself, who planted himself at a courtroom microphone for a solid chunk of the negotiations. By the end of the day, the judge was bending over backwards to encourage the defense to call its intended witnesses, and also offering to reconsider his rulings on permitted testimony.

After all, the government had a great deal of latitude with the witnesses it called to testify, and a reasonable observer might expect the same for the defense. At one point, prosecutor Bevan subpoenaed several dozen people to testify in this case. Apart from opening statements, the entire trial had been devoted to government witnesses thus far, with Bevan continuing to direct his cast of characters well into the afternoon of Day 5.

It was popularly dubbed "snitch day" because the prosecution had scheduled former friends and business associates of Rosenthal to take the stand, and the sensationalism of the event drew a substantial crowd. Courtroom attendance, which was only a sprinkling during the days when law enforcement officers took the witness stand, quickly swelled towards capacity. Those who crowded onto the courtroom's hard wooden pews earned their anticipated glances at the so-called cooperative witnesses...but also ended up with ringside seats to some of the best courtroom drama available in the Northern District of California.

First off, the thrills and danger began well before the jury settled into its box. Defense attorney Robert Amparán was suspiciously side-swiped by a reckless motorist on his way to the courthouse, damaging the pride of his briefcase and causing the lawyer to limp into the courtroom apologetically. In spite of his close call and impaired leg, however, Amparán was deliciously on-point while questioning the government witnesses, who began to flow to the stand just after 8:30am.

Government Witness Henry Rudman

The first of these was Henry Rudman, a 58-year-old realtor who helped Rosenthal acquire the notorious 1419 Mandela Parkway facility. Rudman testified that Rosenthal's wife Jane Klein made the majority of the down payments on the property with money orders and then transferred the title over to her husband. Prosecutor Bevan asked Rudman a series of tense questions designed to establish whether the realtor was aware of a marijuana grow operation in the facility. When Rudman testified that he hadn't been inside the property until after the close of escrow, Bevan's suspicious questions never established whether this was a standard real estate practice. And, all in all, the gems of the prosecutor's examination were disclosures that Rudman had observed the grow operation on Mandela Parkway and had superficially researched a few other potential properties for the defendant. It wasn't thrilling testimony yet, but the day was just warming up.

Photo 16 - Jane Klein and husband Ed Rosenthal by Vanessa Nelson

Through cross-examination of Rudman, the defense finally elicited an estimate of the square footage of 1419 Mandela Parkway. The witness approximated the size at about two thousand square feet.

Amparán's questioning yielded little else of interest, but concluded with warnings that misconduct could lead to the removal of his license to practice real estate in California. "The state can come in and take away the means to your livelihood," Amparán said ominously. "You wouldn't do anything like that, would you?"

"I hope not," Rudman responded before stepping down from the witness stand.

Government Witness Christopher Fay

After so much hinting about the details of an undercover marijuana buy, the prosecutor finally brought DEA Special Agent Chris Fay to the stand. According to his testimony, the agent assumed a fake identity and utilized a confidential informant to gain entry to the 6th Street Harm Reduction Center on January 9th, 2002. Once inside, Fay reported, he purchased approximately 400 marijuana starter plants for a total of $3600 in DEA-provided funds.

The agent testified to seeing former Rosenthal co-defendant Rick Watts at the dispensary during his purchase, but Fay insisted that the man who sold him the marijuana plants was a separate individual named Steve. Bevan then produced from evidence a sales receipt signed by Steve himself, and the prosecutor displayed the exhibit on a courtroom projector while questioning the witness. The receipt listed about a dozen of the strain varieties in the purchase, including Romulan, Champagne, AD 2000, and Tokemon.

Fay testified that before he left the dispensary, Steve gave him detailed instructions about how to bring the plants into a vegetative state. The agent identified notes he had taken on the grow advice, and Bevan pointed to these instructions as evidence that the plants were intended for the manufacture of budding plants.

Amparán took up the cross-examination, eliciting an objection from Bevan within seconds. The defense attorney asked Fay if he was currently working in another state that has medical marijuana laws, but Bevan's objection shut down this line of questioning right away. Also interrupted was Amparán's question about what the DEA agent meant when he testified that he worked as part of the "marijuana group." The defense attorney inquired whether this was an organization that was formed to address California law, but had to move on before he was permitted to get an answer.

Amparán then focused on the false identity Fay assumed when he was infiltrating the Harm Reduction Center – was this character *given* to him, or did the agent *create* the fictional 'Craig?' Upon learning that this identity was invented entirely by Fay, the defense attorney asked what *ailment* Craig suffered from. Bevan was just as vocal as he was in his previous objections, but much less successful.

Photo 17 - Former Harm Reduction Center by Vanessa Nelson

Judge Breyer had the defense rephrase. "Did you know that entry would be limited to people with medical marijuana recommendations?" Amparán asked Fay about the Harm Reduction Center.

The DEA agent said he didn't know, and also denied that he had to get any documentation in order to enter the dispensary. It quickly became clear that if Amparán wanted any references to medical marijuana, he would have to employ more subtlety. Despite a wobbly leg, the defense attorney was up to the job.

Medical comments soon began appearing all over the place in Amparán's questioning, some of them flying in from out of the blue. Asking about the wire Fay wore on undercover missions, the defense attorney inquired whether the agent had encountered any trouble at a dispensary.

"Not in a way that threatened my safety," Fay replied.

"No sick and ailing patients ever tried to chase you out?" Amparán shot back the clever question, with Bevan's objections nipping at its heels.

Amparán took a breather and spent some energy establishing that the witness never saw Rosenthal at the Harm Reduction Center and did not have any evidence that the defendant was involved with the dispensary at all. "You have no knowledge or information about who grew those clones, how they got to the Harm Reduction Center, or how long they were at the Harm Reduction Center before your purchase?"

The defense attorney had no sooner asked the question than the bright-eyed DEA agent confirmed it to be true. As for where they were intended to go, however, that was another matter. "Would it be fair to say that you knew the clones you were purchasing were destined for patients?" Amparán got the whole question out before the prosecutor announced his objection.

This time, the judge excused the jurors from the courtroom. Once they had left, the prosecutor complained that Amparán had asked questions that violated court orders regarding relevant testimony. Bevan didn't dwell on the issue, though, giving it only a passing mention. As it turned out, he had much bigger concerns.

"Rick Watts is not here," the prosecutor reported about his next scheduled witness. "I left a voice mail message to be here by 8:15am, otherwise I would ask your honor to issue an arrest warrant."

Judge Breyer quickly complied with the suggestion. The end of the government's witnesses now in sight, the judge was keen on pushing forward quickly. With all this eagerness, he ordered officers to apprehend Watts and drag him to the witness stand to testify.

Government Witness Robert Martin

The government's penultimate witness, Bob Martin, looked out at the nearly full courtroom and watched the crowd watch him. He was the headliner for the day, and the spectators scrutinized him appropriately. A black pinstripe suit jacket hung over his white t-shirt, casting darkness onto deep-set eyes, a ridged brow, and a frown that later proved itself to be permanent.

As Martin began speaking, swearing his oath and giving his age as 51, the audience noticed his southern accent peeking out. That detail may have helped the jurors to connect him with the ticket scalper from Atlanta that the defense so ominously mentioned during opening statements.

Bevan started in on the examination, asking questions in a manner designed to piece together a picture of the key issues. According to his own testimony, Martin became involved with the Harm Reduction Center in December 2001, and shortly afterward his name was added to a bank account shared by some of the heads of the dispensary. He said severe financial problems arose when one member, Kenneth Hayes, fled to Canada to evade prosecution but continued to withdraw money from the account.

Martin testified that the club had a great deal of debt, and he answered Bevan's questions about a sum of $7000 owed to the defendant by the Harm Reduction Center. Whether this debt was to compensate Rosenthal for plants he provided or to re-pay him for settling up the power bill, Martin claimed not to know. This prompted Bevan to ask if the defendant ever delivered plants to the dispensary himself, and Martin recalled one time when Rosenthal brought 100 plants to the Harm Reduction Center.

But there was evidence someone felt that clones from the Guru of Ganja weren't all they were cracked up to be.

Bevan presented a letter that appeared to be from Rick Watts to Ed Rosenthal, and then the prosecutor read the document aloud to the court. The letter opened with Watts claiming there was a root aphid infestation in a batch of clones Rosenthal had sold to the Harm Reduction Center. It went on to say that the pests had caused substantial damage, for which Watts expected Rosenthal to compensate the dispensary. The letter closed with Watts suggesting the act was intentional, and that Rosenthal had purposefully delivered infected plants in order to undermine the success of other medicinal gardens.

Martin testified to this incident, saying Rosenthal had delivered the clones personally to the club. Upon examination, however, Martin found the clones to be infested, and so he promptly bagged them up for disposal.

The prosecutor submitted as evidence two checks written by Martin to Rosenthal in an effort to reduce the $7000 debt. On the memo portion of one check, the words "consulting fee" were written. Bevan asked why the check would be labeled that way if it was really for plants, but Martin just told the prosecutor, "Mr. Rosenthal told me to." The witness then admitted to feeling dishonest when mislabeling the checks.

As Martin confirmed, however, those two checks never cleared. They were the infamous stopped-payment checks that led to a small claims suit filed by Rosenthal against Martin in 2004.

When Bevan started questioning Martin about the civil case, however, Judge Breyer cut him off right away. "Whatever happened in small claims court, that's not relevant here," the judge declared. Bevan had nothing further.

Sedate during the government's questioning, Martin's emotions roared to life when Amparán stepped up to cross-examine him. It was then that another personality emerged, and it turned out to be an angry and vitriolic one that placed enormous blame on the defense attorneys personally.

The defense team's concern about Martin was that he was being protected from prosecution by authorities that needed him as a witness. Such protection, they argued, allowed Martin to engage in lawless and immoral behavior without any legal consequences.

In a pre-trial motion, the defense asked to be given IRS tax returns on all government witnesses. They felt sure that some of these witnesses were not paying taxes, and that the U.S. Attorney was purposefully ignoring tax evasion by the cooperative witnesses.

The defense team mentioned Martin specifically when they argued this motion, alleging that he ran two medical marijuana clubs without paying taxes. Then, on the eve of his scheduled testimony in the Rosenthal re-trial, the medical marijuana community was abuzz with news that Martin had voluntarily closed down both of his dispensaries.

Martin did not shy away from this topic during the cross-examination. In fact, he brought it up, and aggressively too, almost as soon as Amparán began questioning him.

The defense attorney started out by asking Martin if he had been operating a marijuana dispensary in conflict with federal law but without federal sanction.

"Yes, I was operating a clinic, not selling it myself, until just recently, when I had to close based on harassment from your law firm," Martin spit out gruffly. "When your law firm turned us in to the federal government, it caused much harassment."

It was off on a bad foot, and it didn't get any friendlier when Amparán suggested that the reason for Martin's harassment was because he has been characterized as a snitch within the medical marijuana community.

The court required Amparán to rephrase his question for the record without the word 'snitch,' and this seemed to calm things down for a few minutes as Martin seethed on other subjects. When the defense asked if he had another building that he wanted to turn into a dispensary in 2002, he grumbled, "I was tired of fighting with the one in the ghetto."

The defense also asked about the letter detailing the alleged root aphid infestation, and implied that Martin could have written it to make it appear as though it had been authored by Watts. Amparán suggested that Martin might have done this in order to deliberately spark conflict between Watts and Rosenthal. By distracting these two players with a quarrel, the defense attorney hypothesized, Martin would be able to get full control of the dispensary to himself.

"Absolutely not!" Martin seemed outraged, then genuinely tickled. He laughed a great deal, displaying a mocking disdain. "I was afraid to enter that building, it was in such a bad location."

But Amparán was focused on the letter, and on the motivation for writing it. "Would it be fair to say that the clones came in and the clones were fine, but you just didn't want to pay for them, so you stole them?"

Martin called the theory an absolute lie, but Amparán cited recent incidents where the witness lashed out through vengefully personal attacks. "Yesterday, did you call my law office repeatedly and ask my secretary repeatedly about how my law office was putting you out of business?" the defense attorney demanded. "And made similar calls to Green Aid and left those messages?"

Martin said he had a good reason for the phone calls. "I wanted them to know that Mr. Rosenthal has closed down two clubs."

"Is Mr. Rosenthal the *only* vendor you haven't paid?" Amparán asked, still just warming up. "Is it true that you use your connection to Mr. Bevan to go around shaking down the community?"

The defense attorney then suggested that Martin doesn't need to pay people back because he knows he isn't going to get in trouble with the law.

Those were fighting words, and Martin was irate. "I think you can be arrested for what you just said," he challenged.

Judge Breyer broke in on the heated exchange. "Mr. Amparán is not going to jail for what he just said," the judge assured the wide-eyed audience and jury.

It seemed a good enough place to end the cross-examination, so Judge Breyer excused Martin from the stand and allowed the jurors to take a break.

Once the jury box had emptied, Amparán turned to the judge and addressed disparaging remarks Martin had made to defense attorney Shari Greenberger that morning. "That he called Ms. Greenberger a drag queen goes to his bias," Amparán insisted.

Greenberger then stood up for herself and spoke about the claims. "He has made statements every time I walk out of the courtroom," she said of Martin. "I want the record to reflect my fear."

"He thinks he has the protection of the federal government to do whatever he wants," Amparán speculated. It was an argument the defense had put forward many times with regard to Martin.

Photo 18 - Shari Greenberger
by Vanessa Nelson

But suddenly Bevan's news took priority – in the time it took for Bob Martin to testify, Rick Watts had been found, taken into custody, and brought to the courthouse. The long arm of the law had snatched him up and delivered him to the witness stand, in front of a crowd of curious onlookers.

Government Witness Richard Watts

A familiar figure in this case, Rick Watts was formerly Ed Rosenthal's co-defendant. A spine-shattering car accident prevented him from standing trial alongside his old associate in 2003, but Watts was nonetheless remembered and included when the federal government filed its superseding indictment last year. The charges mostly slid off of him, but what remained took a plea deal to remove. The courthouse was no stranger to Watts, but in spite of all the implied familiarity, Watts seemed somehow alienated. Being a witness for the prosecution, however reluctantly, seldom wins any friends in the marijuana advocacy crowd. Still, Watts entered the courtroom looking like he didn't have a friend in all the world.

His hair was disheveled, his breathing heavy, his gaze pained, and he shook visibly in his seat. While waiting for the jury to be summoned, Amparán came over to Watts and sat beside him for a minute. "How're you doing?" the defense attorney asked in a whisper. "Did they treat you okay?" Watts just maintained his vacant stare, and then shook his head a few times.

The court came back into session and the tardy Watts took his place on the witness stand. His seat was the perfect height to showcase the Americans for Safe Access shirt he was wearing, which read "Defend Medical Marijuana." At first, he seemed unable to follow the prosecutor's instructions, but eventually lucidity began to return. Bevan wanted it on record that cooperating with witness testimony had *not* been part of the plea deal Watts accepted on his tax evasion charges, and through a series of questions answered by Watts, the point became very clear to the court.

The prosecutor then turned his attention to the Harm Reduction Center, which Watts testified to starting up with Kenneth Hayes in 1999. The company bank account had been established by the year 2000, as evidenced by a signature card for the account presented from evidence. Watts easily identified the names on that card, no doubt inspiring the confidence of the prosecutor.

Such confidences, however, were quite premature. For the remainder of the examination, Watts blocked Bevan at every turn. His answers skillfully shut down each line of questioning while simultaneously emphasizing the medical nature of what had previously been called 'marijuana dispensaries.'

Whenever Bevan presented the witness with a check, invariably Watts related that check to construction expenses. Even the checks with the word "payroll" in the memo line were really construction-related, as Watts explained on the stand. That notation just meant that volunteers would help the Harm Reduction Center build things, and the club would write a check to reimburse them for the materials they purchased. Any kind of attempt at a real payroll would be a joke, according to Watts. "The Harm Reduction Center never had any money, *ever*."

Thinking he could bust up the carpentry party, Bevan brought up a series of checks payable in cash, in amounts between $3000-$5000. Predictably, though, the witness claimed these were construction expenses. "We were building, and everything happens so fast when you're building like that," Watts said, beginning to relax slightly. "I wouldn't remember those checks. I just wrote them as fast as I needed the materials."

Ever persistent, Bevan brought in a series of checks that he believed were "used to pay for marijuana from vendors that was intended for resale." Watts, of course, disagreed with Bevan's theory on the purpose.

But Bevan had a trick up his sleeve – the memo fields of the checks contained various entries he had reason to believe were the names of regular vendors for the Harm Reduction Center. "What about Bart?" Bevan asked. "Isn't one of the vendors nicknamed Bart?"

Watts gave him nothing. "I wasn't involved with the vendors," he said. "I just did construction."

Bevan grew insistent in his tone as he continued to quiz Watts on the various names. At one point, Bevan asked about the notation "pineapple," and the frustration of his task compounded with a growing sense of urgency. Soon he seemed like a raving madman, "Pineapple! It says: Pineapple! Don't you recall a lady by the name of Pineapple?!"

Watts said simply, casually, "No…that's a *fruit*."

It was all in the delivery, and it struck the spectators' funny bones quite skillfully. The courtroom collectively giggled, but the prosecutor was not so amused. "So you were constantly building?" he asked in a skeptical tone.

"There was a danger factor -- a safety factor," Watts explained. "People were stoned, you know."

Bevan pushed forward, "But isn't it fair to say that the Harm Reduction Center acquired marijuana from various vendors for resale?"

"I wouldn't know about that. That's not my job," Watts said coolly. "My job was to build and to keep people safe."

The witness was able to point the defendant out in the courtroom, but Watts certainly couldn't confirm that Rosenthal sold marijuana to the Harm Reduction Center. It was a stance that threatened the government's case, and the prosecutor appeared duly frustrated. "Is that your testimony – that you don't know if Mr. Rosenthal sold marijuana to the Harm Reduction Center?"

Watts affirmed the statement, "I didn't pay much attention to what was going on," he added. "I spent more time running back and forth between Home Depot than anything else."

But Bevan was a man of preparation. He pulled out the exhibit he showed Bob Martin earlier – the letter allegedly written by Watts, which explicitly spoke of the Harm Reduction Center buying clones from the defendant. Bevan looked triumphant as he began to rattle off questions about the letter, but the smile didn't last long. As soon as the prosecutor asked who typed the letter, the game was on. "It was one of the patients," Watts replied.

Bevan caught on quickly – to ask more questions would mean incessant mentions of patients in front of the jury. At one point, Watts answered a question about the letter by saying, "Patients run the club. You have to understand that was the design of the clubs."

Bevan, however, had an ace up his sleeve. "Would it surprise you to learn that this was taken from your computer at your home?" he asked slyly.

Watts did not seem surprised in the least. "I took the computer because they owed me money," he said matter-of-factly.

Admitting to theft was a clever distraction, but Bevan didn't take the bait. Instead, Watts ended up explaining what would motivate a patient to write such a letter, while at the same time slowly chipping away at the sales charges against Rosenthal. "The plants were donated," he told the prosecutor. "If people were unhappy, that was probably why."

At times the prosecutor would get going on a roll, only to be foiled at the very end.

He asked if marijuana was sold on a regular basis at the Harm Reduction Center, and Watts confirmed this. "But you took the marijuana, didn't you?" Bevan asked.

The witness's reply to the accusation was worded simply but powerfully. "I have a lot of pain," Watts said.

Bevan then changed the subject, deciding to focus next on the raid of the witness's home on February 12th, 2002. "They took everything I own," Watts said of the federal agents who searched his residence and his vehicle. The comment inspired looks of concern from the jury.

The prosecutor, however, had something to prove. He presented Exhibit 79, a folder of checks from the Harm Reduction Center. Before Bevan could begin questioning, however, something distracted him.

Over and over again, the prosecutor brought the folder up to his nose and sniffed, enthralled. "This still smells like marijuana, doesn't it?" He said it again, placing the folder on the witness stand and awaiting a response.

Watts was not as interested in the lingering aroma as the prosecutor, but he obligingly answered Bevan's questions about the checks. When asked why he was in possession of the checkbook, Watts explained that he had it in order to buy building materials. The same reason explained the $5000 found at his home during the raid.

It seemed that Bevan was getting nowhere fast while questioning Watts about *items*, so the prosecutor switched his tactics and started asking about *people*. Predictably, Watts said that he was so engaged in construction that he barely knew who was at the Harm Reduction Center. He did know Bob Martin, but since they worked in separate spheres, Watts had no information to offer about Bob's activities. "Bob's business is money," Watts said in typically plain style. "That's what he does."

Bevan tried a few more names before giving up. He asked Watts if he knew Brian Lundeen, but the prosecutor came up empty-handed.

"George, you gotta understand something," Watts said, conspicuously addressing the prosecutor by his first name. "The social circle that was going on there, I didn't pay any attention."

At that, Bevan ended his questioning and gave the witness over to Amparán for cross-examination.

As the defense took over, it colored in the picture outlined by the direct examination. Watts was characterized as a hapless repairman who got left holding the bag when one of the dispensary operators fled the country and drained the bank accounts. The scenario sounded almost like a pitch for a sitcom.

In this version of the story, Watts took over management to the best of his ability, signing checks because he was the only one who could. About the typed letter accusing Rosenthal of selling pest-laden plants, Watts testified that it employed phrases he wouldn't use and also confessed, "I wasn't very good on a computer."

Amparán asked if Rosenthal was authorized to do anything at the Harm Reduction Center, and Watts told him, "Not unless he was involved with the patients, no."

Next, Amparán focused on the witness's reluctance to testify. "You aren't happy to be here, are you?" the defense attorney asked. "In fact, you were brought here against your will."

Watts agreed, and Judge Breyer jumped in quickly. "The jury should know that I directed he be brought here," the judge explained in regard to Watts. "It was an order of the court, not the government."

That clarified, Amparán moved on to elucidate a few more issues. He asked if Watts had ever sold marijuana products offsite from the dispensary, and Watts shook his head. He also denied any involvement in the undercover sale to Christopher Fay.

"I was not a budtender," Watts said. "I am not a budtender."

With that, Amparán ended the cross-examination. The witness was excused and the jury left the courtroom for the day.

The Defense Rests

Judge Breyer was shaken by what happened next. Having gone through the prosecution's witnesses, it was time for the defense to present its case...but instead, they simply declined to do so.

"Based on the conclusion of yesterday's session, I think we are going to rest," Amparán said amiably. His comment referred to decisions made after the jury was excused on Day 4, when Judge Breyer denied and restricted the testimony of many of the defense's witnesses.

"The issues we want to address are issues the court has barred," Amparán explained. "We will rest and say the government has not met its burden."

"There is some evidence that is relevant based on review," the judge suggested, looking concerned. "You could call Jane Klein."

But that wasn't enough to satisfy the defense. "You have either precluded or limited evidence, so that we would look foolish if we presented [the witnesses]," Amparán told the judge.

"I want a record on this," Judge Breyer insisted, getting anxious. "I am not precluding you. I don't know whether you would look foolish or not, but if there's a conviction and a review by an appellate court, I don't want to leave the record with the view that I'm precluding you."

Amparán still refused. "We would have a battle in court in front of witnesses and with the jury present," he surmised. Based on the nature of the proceedings during the previous week, his prediction seemed quite believable.

Judge Breyer appeared uncomfortable at the idea, and was worried enough to offer new consideration of all proposed witnesses. "All previous rulings, I'm now setting aside," he declared. "I will listen to an offer of proof to any witnesses you would like to call."

The one restriction: testimony about the medical aspects of marijuana would still be irrelevant.

At that, Rosenthal was outraged enough to jump into the discussion himself. "I am being selected out because of my advocacy," he claimed. "I would like to continue the case with the witnesses we originally wanted to call."

The judge then inquired if Rosenthal would testify, and his question was treated like an open invitation for personal criticism from the defendant. "I would testify before *the jury*, not before *you*," Rosenthal began. "I believe you are prejudiced. I believe you should step down. I believe this is a mistrial!"

But the defendant's scathing comments were not limited to the judge. "The government has been in a RICO situation with Mr. Bevan," Rosenthal said in reference to the Racketeer Influenced and Corrupt Organizations Act, which allows harsher sentences for crimes committed as part of an ongoing criminal organization.

Even after the defendant's outburst of accusations, Judge Breyer still urged him to take the witness stand. The judge sweetened the deal offering Rosenthal unrestricted testimony. As for the other witnesses, the judge wanted to know who would be called. He balked when Amparán suggested Supervisor Nate Miley, and asked about the subject of Miley's testimony.

Rosenthal was more than happy to answer the question himself. "He would say that I'm an officer of the city and allowed by the city to grow marijuana and provide it to the patients, and that the city attorney said I was free from prosecution," the defendant said heatedly.

The judge was dismissive, sticking to his previous suggestion. "You can testify about anything you want to," Judge Breyer offered the defendant. "Whether or not it's admissible, you can testify to it. But the testimony of corroborating witnesses is inadmissible."

Rosenthal's response was to propose calling Bevan as a witness. Tolerant, the judge asked what the prosecutor would testify about, and Rosenthal requested that Bevan not know the topics of the examination. "You can make the offer of proof outside Mr. Bevan's presence," the judge acquiesced.

But the defendant staunchly demanded corroborating witnesses, and declared that it was an injustice to be deprived of them. "I am not going to play in this kangaroo charade court!" he exclaimed. "It's like Stalinist Soviet Russia. Why don't we just call me 'comrade' and send me off to hang?"

As the suggestion was rhetorical, no one answered. Bevan stood with his hands in his pockets and looked down.

"Smiles, smirks, nasty expressions go to the jury without being admonished. That shows what kind of court this is," Rosenthal continued, turning again to address the judge personally. "I know by your previous actions that you are working with the prosecutor, hand-in-hand!"

Judge Breyer was done listening to vague accusations. "If you have any evidence of government misconduct, please provide me with such information, because I don't know about it," he requested.

The judge then announced that he had received a note from a juror, which, amongst other questions, asked how this case could be brought in *California*. Judge Breyer handed the note to both sides, stressing that his instructions to the jury would be to consider federal law only.

Bevan's solution was simple. "This speaks to the public misunderstanding," he said. "I agree that federal law controls in this case, but the defendant's grow did not conform with California law either. If the jury could be told this, it could be beneficial."

In conclusion, Bevan explained, "When there's medical marijuana lurking, there's a red flag up, and people don't know the details."

In spite of the prosecutor's argument, Judge Breyer was not inclined to discuss with the jury whether Rosenthal had been in compliance with state law or not. "It's not a question of whether people have gotten it right or wrong," the judge said about medical marijuana. "It's about whether it's relevant, and the court has ruled that it's not relevant. Not a lot of people understand it. That's not the issue here."

That said, the judge wanted to know whether the defense would present its case or not. Rosenthal made an attempt to answer, but Judge Breyer told him flatly to let his lawyers speak for him. "I am not asking Mr. Rosenthal. I am asking his attorneys."

Amparán took on that duty, saying, "Every time the court makes a statement, I am more secure in the decision to rest."

Nonetheless, the judge still gave the defense a night to sleep on it, and would expect a final answer at 8am the next morning.

It seemed time to adjourn, but Bevan still had a complaint. He was upset that the defense had maligned his witnesses during the opening statements, calling them liars and thieves, wife beaters and drug addicts. It was a complaint the prosecutor raised frequently during the past week, and repetition only resulted in the same answer.

First off, Judge Breyer claimed that most jurors don't remember the opening statements. Secondly, the judge assured the prosecutor that he would advise the jury that opening statements are not evidence. And, finally, Judge Breyer reminded Bevan that he was free to present his side during closing arguments.

But the prosecutor, unsatisfied, simply mumbled the refrain, "They put strong labels on our witnesses."

After court adjourned, observers gathered in the hallway to congratulate Rosenthal on his compelling speech. They were still crowded there when Bevan emerged from the courtroom, and Rosenthal lit up when he spotted the prosecutor. "Let's hear it for him!" Rosenthal shouted, and the group was eager to oblige.

Bevan walked alone down the hallway to the elevators, the sounds of sarcastic applause following him the whole way.

Wednesday, May 23rd, 2007
Protesters Flock

It came as no surprise to courtroom spectators when Ed Rosenthal announced he was sticking to his plan to rest his case without calling any witnesses. Although Judge Breyer had requested he take some time to sleep on the decision, a night of meditation on the issue appeared to do nothing but strengthen Rosenthal's resolve. In an early morning session, held prior to the entry of the jurors, he announced to the court that he had no case to present unless he was allowed to call corroborating witnesses. "I will testify," Rosenthal offered, "but only if I can bring any witnesses I want, without a proffer."

Just days before the trial began, Judge Breyer made a series of strict rulings barring the testimony of many of the defense's intended witnesses. In addition to excluding patient witnesses who could testify to the medical efficacy of marijuana, the judge also denied the testimony of Alameda County Supervisor Nate Miley. In Judge Breyer's view, Miley had nothing relevant to say on the stand. To the defense, however, he was an ace in the hole, since he would be giving testimony that Rosenthal had been deputized by the City of Oakland to supply medical marijuana to dispensaries.

Rosenthal stood firm on his position that Miley be permitted to testify, but the defendant also called for another set of witnesses. "Bring in the former jurors!" Rosenthal demanded during the Wednesday morning session. "They feel very passionate about this."

Indeed they do. As most followers of the saga know, the jurors from Rosenthal's first trial revolted when they learned that they had convicted him without being allowed to hear testimony about his deputization or about the medical nature of the marijuana. The idea that Judge Breyer would restrict this information again during the re-trial only strengthened Rosenthal's belief that the judge was on the side of the prosecution.

"You're working for the government!" Rosenthal accused the judge. "You are not acting like an independent justice. You are acting like a prosecutor!

"When I first came into this courtroom, you looked at me like I was a common criminal," Rosenthal continued, describing the beginning of his prosecution in 2002. "You had a look of disdain. Everyone noted it."

Now that he has proven himself to be respectable, Rosenthal argued, it was time for everyone to behave honorably. In his view, this meant that the judge should voluntarily step down from the case.

Concluding his plea, Rosenthal said loudly and boldly to Judge Breyer, "We would like you to recuse yourself, and we would like to have a hearing on it."

The judge was unwilling to address many of the demands laid before him, and his response to Rosenthal's monologue was quite sedate. "I'm going to interpret that as a statement by the defendant that he does not wish to testify because I will not allow certain witnesses who will testify about evidence I have already ruled is inadmissible."

Judge Breyer then took up another concern. He had reason to believe that the prosecutor had altered an exhibit before presenting it as evidence.

At issue was the document shown to the court when Bevan was questioning witness Bob Martin about his civil suit with Rosenthal. The judge had noticed the exhibit presented at that time was incomplete, lacking much of the information that had been present when the document was initially admitted as evidence.

Bevan, however, denied all claims of tampering, and hinted that his choice to submit only the relevant information to the witness was somehow a strategic one. In any case, Bevan argued, he had submitted complete evidence as it pertained to the subject matter of the questioning. "I only asked Mr. Martin if he had been sued," the prosecutor explained, "and to that extent I provided full evidence."

Judge Breyer appeared satisfied by the explanation, and turned next to address an old but lingering issue in the case – what to do about the witnesses who were refusing to testify? The judge had delayed answering that question as long as he possibly could, waiting until the government had presented its cooperative witnesses before making a decision.

To defense attorney Robert Amparán, the solution seemed simple – no action was needed at all. "What could be the benefit from additional testimony of immunized witnesses?" he asked incredulously.

The government, however, was resolute. "We're going to pursue it, your honor," Bevan told the judge. "We're going to go forward and call the witnesses we want to call."

Amparán was quick to inquire about what would happen if the witnesses *all* refused to testify, but Judge Breyer provided no firm answers. "If they refuse to testify, then I have to figure out what the appropriate remedy is."

The uncooperative witnesses and their attorneys were then scheduled to report to the courtroom on Friday, May 25th. Since the hearing would take place outside the jury's presence and since the case couldn't move forward until this issue was resolved, jurors received the happy news that they would be getting a five-day weekend. They would not be needed again until the next

Tuesday, at which time they were likely to hear closing arguments.

But before being given the case, the jury would receive detailed instructions on many issues. As Judge Breyer spoke on this subject, he referenced the note from the juror that asked how the federal government could bring this case to trial in the state of California.

The judge then explained how he would answer the question for the jury. "I will tell them, 'As to medical marijuana, state and local laws regarding it are irrelevant, immaterial and cannot be considered by you in your deliberations.'"

The judge continued reciting his jury instructions on this matter, "'Federal law prohibits the manufacture and distribution of marijuana. This is the law everywhere in the United States. When there is conflict between state and local law on one hand, and federal law on one hand, the federal law trumps the local and state law. Federal law is the law that governs you in this courtroom and governs me. State law, whatever the state law is, is not relevant.'"

It was a stark reminder to the judge that he had many points to emphasize to the jurors before they began their deliberations. For the defense, it was proof that the jurors were at least vaguely aware of the contentious federalist issues that the court had prevented them from hearing about. And for the government, it was yet another ill omen.

Early on, Bevan had been dismayed to discover that volunteers had been handing out leaflets about jury nullification outside the courthouse. But the prosecutor's blood boiled over when he arrived at the courthouse well before 8am that morning, and discovered an activist group already hanging up a banner near one of the entrances.

"I see the lady in the courtroom now. I saw her today, hanging a banner outside," Bevan said with dramatic emphasis, eyeing activist organizer Shona Gochenaur as she sat in the audience seats. Downstairs, on the Golden Gate side of the courthouse, her banner was still hanging and being tended by her activist group, Axis of Love.

Photo 19 - Axis of Love banner prosecutor Bevan objected to
by Vanessa Nelson

Amparán pointed out that this was on the "state side" of the courthouse, facing administrative buildings for the State of California, but that detail did nothing to put Bevan's worries to rest.

"The government may want to keep the jurors dumb, deaf and blind," Amparán continued, "but there's only a certain amount of prophylactic action that can be taken to keep them dumb, deaf and blind."

Judge Breyer turned to Bevan and assured him that the jury would be instructed to disregard banners and leaflets. "What did the sign say?" he asked the prosecutor.

Bevan struggled to recall the exact wording, but approximated as best he could. "'We Care – Support Medical Marijuana.'"

The defense failed to see this as such a grave threat, and made sarcastic suggestions about the penalties that should be given to

Gochenaur. "Maybe we should shackle and flog her," Amparán suggested in a deadpan, before turning to his own commentary. "It's amazing when the government is afraid of the truth."

"Those kinds of comments are not very helpful, Mr. Amparán," the judge said sternly.

The prosecutor saw this expression of disapproval as his opening to discuss other controversial comments made by the defense. This time, however, it was purely personal.

"Mr. Rosenthal has said some things to me," Bevan began. "He called me a coward in the courtroom. He followed me down the hallway calling me a coward. When I leave the courtroom, there's a crowd and he's inciting them… That behavior is uncalled for and personal attacks are uncalled for."

Judge Breyer emphasized the need for respect and dignity, but as for the nature of the words themselves, he was fairly relaxed. "Mr. Rosenthal is free to say what he wants to say," the judge said matter-of-factly. "He may be highly critical of the court, he may be highly critical of the federal government, and he may be highly critical of this prosecution – that's his right."

Encouraged by the judge's language, the defendant stood up and bounded across the room. "Can I call him a coward? I just want to know, because he *is* a coward!" Rosenthal made his inquiry zealously, first referencing the prosecutor and then turning to address him directly, "And you're a tattletale and a crybaby!"

"The court has a responsibility to make sure there is decorum," Judge Breyer asserted. "This should at least be the subject of discussion between counsel and defendant."

But as for personal scolding, the judge was well aware of the limits of his effectiveness. "I am not restricting your client's free speech," he admitted to the defense attorneys. "I think an admonition on Mr. Rosenthal would be useless."

It may well have been one of the wisest things Judge Breyer said all day.

The court then adjourned early, in anticipation of Friday's hearing on the uncooperative witnesses.

If Bevan made his way outside at lunchtime, however, he would have seen that the lone banner of the morning's dismay had bloomed into a large gathering with dozens of activists, signs galore, and a boisterous bullhorn. Since the prosecutor had been so intensely irked by the presence of one discreet banner, then the protest must have provoked nothing short of a apoplectic fit.

Photo 20 - May 23 protestors gathered outside the court building
by Vanessa Nelson

Photo 21 - Ed Rosenthal addresses the crowd by Tim Castleman

Photo 22 - ASA Rep Steph Sherer
by Tim Castleman

Photo 23 - Axis of Love protestor
by Tim Castleman

Photo 24 - Ed Rosenthal with a few friends by Tim Castleman

Photo 25 - Line of protestors by Tim Castleman

Photo 26 - Ed Rosenthal speaking to crowd by Tim Castleman

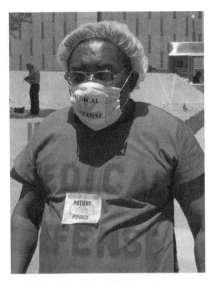

Photo 27 - Axis of Love protestor
by Tim Castleman

Photo 28 - Protestors wore masks with
'Medical Defense' printed on them
by Tim Castleman

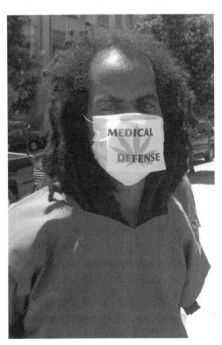

Photo 29 - Protestors wore medical
worker uniforms by Tim Castleman

Photo 30 - Emotions ran high
by Tim Castleman

Friday, May 25th, 2007
Uncooperative Witnesses

If one day in the Ed Rosenthal re-trial could be marked as the most inspirational, May 25th would stand alone as the winner. On this day, six brave men and women took a stand against the federal government, risking their freedom in order to follow their vision of truth and justice. In front of the court, they remained undeterred by threats of imprisonment, and instead used the opportunity to articulate their beliefs with compelling eloquence...

The presentation of the government's case was at its conclusion, and the court took a day to deal with those witnesses who had been subpoenaed by the prosecution but refused to testify. Judge Breyer's approach had been to deal with these uncooperative witnesses only as necessary, by first letting the government call its compliant witnesses and then evaluating whether or not additional testimony was needed. It was a practical approach, but one that kept everyone in suspense.

As a result, the fate of the recalcitrant witnesses was a concern that lingered silently underneath the proceedings. Only after two weeks of trial was that underlying anxiety addressed, as each witness was questioned by the judge and went on record as refusing to testify. One after another, in an inspiring show of strength and courage, these witnesses came to the stand and boldly articulated the reasons for their resistance.

In doing so, these individuals faced enormous personal peril. Not only did they give up the offer of immunity that came with testifying, but they also put themselves in jeopardy of incurring penalties resulting from their refusal. Over and over, the judge reiterated the consequences of contempt: jail, fines, and additional prosecution. But each time the penalties were listed, the witnesses readily accepted them. Their stance was selfless, righteous, and truly heroic.

Recalcitrant Witness Jeffrey Jones

A few witnesses were excused right off the bat, including Anthony Lopez, Lu Saechao, and Vince Brown. Yet another, Kathleen Capetti, had been allowed to go on vacation, but her attorney Laurence Lichter promised to get in touch with her over the weekend. Right away, the list of uncooperative witnesses was substantially reduced. The one wobbler, in the judge's view, was Oakland Cannabis Buyers Club proprietor Jeff Jones.

Photo 31 - Jeff Jones
by Vanessa Nelson

Although a long-established figure in the medical marijuana movement, Jones fails miserably at cutting the figure of a typical forefather or pioneer. With an endearing face, a delightfully impish grin, and an "aww, shucks" sort of demeanor, Jones looks every bit the part of the charming but mischievous youth. If not entirely innocent-looking, he carries the air of being guilty only of pranks with a slingshot or of swiping a freshly-baked pie from a windowsill.

"I'm not convinced that this person ought to testify," Judge Breyer said while eyeing Jones. "Not because it's not cumulative

– all of his testimony is cumulative – I'm just not convinced that this is the witness who ought to testify to these things."

Jones's situation, at least on the legal level, happens to be more complicated than that of the other uncooperative witnesses. As his attorney told the court, Jones is currently a party in another case: United States v. OCBC. Presented with this information, Judge Breyer considered whether involvement in this other case would somehow interfere with the testimony Jones would give in the Rosenthal trial.

"He does have a horse in the race on the civil aspects," the judge mused, eventually deciding against compelling Jones to testify.

As the excused witness beat a quick path to the door, Judge Breyer commented, "There are other witnesses here who could testify to what he will testify to."

But if the judge really expected the remaining witnesses to fill in the blanks, he would be woefully disappointed.

Recalcitrant Witness Etienne Fontan

The first to take the stand was Etienne Fontan, a young man in

Photo 32 - Etienne Fontan
by Vanessa Nelson

a dark suit who radiated calm confidence. When asked to swear to God in his oath, Fontan replied politely, "I don't believe in God, but I will still affirm."

It was the first sign that this witness held his beliefs and his discourse very seriously, and observers took keen notice of this behavior. Self-assured and poised, Fontan went on to handle his examination in a

109

way that demonstrated to the entire courtroom the definition of integrity.

First off, U.S. Attorney George Bevan, Jr., asked whether Fontan had been employed by Rosenthal. The inquiry met with immediate resistance.

"With respect to the court, your honor, and as a U.S. citizen and veteran of this country, I see no reason to answer any of these questions," Fontan declared, loudly and clearly. "I cannot proceed with the answering of any of your questions."

Bevan went on to summarize what the government asserted the testimony would reveal, if the witness had agreed to testify fully and truthfully. According to the prosecutor, Fontan had been an employee of Rosenthal at 1419 Mandela Parkway, and had been involved in the manufacture and distribution of marijuana from that facility. By refusing to testify, Fontan was depriving the court of information regarding the activities of other employees at that location. As such, Bevan asked that the judge find Fontan to be in contempt and impose appropriate sanction.

Judge Breyer reminded the witness that he would be given immunity for his testimony, but Fontan was still unswayed. The judge then detailed the possible consequences of contempt, including indefinite time in jail, unspecified financial penalty, and the possibility of an indictment being filed against him. Knowing these conditions, Fontan was given another opportunity to agree to testify.

"As a sovereign American citizen, I disagree with this court's actions," Fontan began. "I stand firm in my belief not to answer the questions... I have been a product of this system before in the military. I understand about incarceration and what the government can do to me. I have been a subject as its guinea pig as a Gulf War veteran, and suffered because of it."

The spectators were absorbed, their attention rapt.

"There is nothing you can do to change my mind," Fontan concluded. "I stand firmly in my belief."

When he stepped down from the stand, it was obvious that a certain standard of moral precision had been set. Fontan, head held high, led the way in exemplifying a staunch but dignified opposition to the court's attempts to impose belief and coerce behavior.

Recalcitrant Witness Brian Lundeen

Courtroom observers had heard much of Brian Lundeen during the days before he took the stand. Over the course of the re-trial, the prosecutor had speculated on multiple occasions about Lundeen's involvement in the case. In the process of doing so, Bevan had read off Lundeen's phone number to the court, and also displayed a copy of Lundeen's driver's license on the courtroom projector for all to see. If the fair-haired young man had a sense of being over-exposed, he came by it honestly.

Once Lundeen was sworn in on the stand, however, he encountered the same familiar questions that greeted the other witnesses.

When asked if he was aware of the immunity order, Lundeen was frank, "Apparently nothing I say in the case can be used to help Ed Rosenthal, so I'm absolutely going to refuse."

He showed a similar, well-reasoned resistance when questioned about whether he had been Rosenthal's employee. "I'd love to tell the whole truth and nothing but the truth," Lundeen said plainly, "but if you make me swear that, and then refuse to let me do it, you'd be asking me to commit a crime."

Prosecutor Bevan then laid out the details of what he believed Lundeen's testimony would reveal, if it were given freely and truthfully. According to the government, this witness worked at the Mandela Parkway facility to manufacture marijuana, and he distributed marijuana at various locations with the defendant.

Lundeen then received from the judge the standard reminders about immunity and warnings about contempt, but he was resolute in his decision not to testify. "I have already stated that I'm not going to cooperate with the prosecution," Lundeen told the judge. He then added, respectfully, that he was not doing this to disobey the judge, but merely to follow the path he believed to be right. With the dignity of the righteous, Lundeen stepped down from the stand.

Recalcitrant Witness Evan Schwartz

Readers well versed in the Rosenthal re-trial were already familiar with the name of Evan Schwartz. His father Gary was the second of the prosecution's witnesses to take the stand, testifying that Evan Schwartz had been driving a vehicle that was observed during DEA surveillance on Rosenthal's Mandela Parkway property.

His father may have given testimony against him, but this honorable young man refused to give testimony against *anyone*. He greeted every attempt to procure information with the same response, "I respectfully refuse to answer this question."

His position remained solid even when Bevan read off the description of what his testimony would reveal. According to the prosecutor, this witness contributed fully with the manufacture of marijuana at the Mandela Parkway facility, drove a car that was observed during DEA surveillance at that location, and was the Evan who was mentioned on the "to do list" recovered from the premises during the raid.

After being given the requisite cautioning about the consequences of his choice, Evan Schwartz stood by his principles. "Respectfully, I do not wish to answer any questions," he told the court.

Amongst the more stoic of the witnesses, his answers embodied an elegant simplicity that was pure in its composition and rich in its strength.

Recalcitrant Witness Deborah Goldsberry

Veteran activist Debby Goldsberry is widely revered for her dedication and passion, and she brought both of these with her to the witness stand. It was a challenge that had a visible emotional effect on her, and Goldsberry managed to channel her feelings into a compelling commentary that concluded with her heartfelt pleas for compassion.

When Goldsberry was called to the stand, observers cast their eyes on a fair-haired woman who moved with equal measure of grace and purpose. She appeared to have the full virtues of beauty, but without any of its frailties or pretensions. And like a medium for the mood, all the gravity of the situation showed clearly on her face as she took her oath.

At first, she conveyed a sense of bewilderment and frustration, disclosing that she never received notice of this hearing. Beyond that, she was unable to discern basic but crucial facts from the summons she did receive. "Nothing has been clear," Goldsberry said of her subpoena.

When asked if she understood that she was being offered immunity for her testimony, she replied with a hint of exasperation, "Not exactly, but I'll take your word for it."

On that shaky ground, the prosecutor jumped right into his inquiries, asking Goldsberry if she had purchased a quantity of marijuana from an employee of the defendant.

The witness promptly declined to answer and asserted that she was invoking her 5th Amendment right. "I think this prosecution is against the will of the people," she said with conviction into her microphone. "It's against the will of the citizens, and it's actually *harming* the citizens of California. I believe it would be illegal and immoral for me to participate in this prosecution because of that."

The witness then took the bold step of personally addressing the judge and the prosecutor. "I know deep in your hearts you both share that same view," Goldsberry continued. "Mr. Bevan, I know that you are upset and taking this very personally, but Judge Breyer, I know you are a good man and you know this is right."

The judge, at this point in the process, was required to remind Goldsberry that an order of immunity applied to her testimony. In light of her comments about the 5th Amendment, however, Judge Breyer felt it was necessary to describe the situation more fully. He told Goldsberry that the 5th Amendment only provides protection from self-incrimination, a possibility that is effectively prevented by the order of immunity. "From the court's point of view, you have no privilege against self-incrimination once I sign an order compelling you to testify under a grant of immunity," the judge explained.

It was a revelation that startled many in the audience, provoking whispers and head-shaking.

The witness, for her part, was looking towards the future. "As much as I respect the court, I can't wait until you guys are on our side of this thing," Goldsberry said to the judge and prosecutor. "I am a good citizen. I support my community. What I don't support is what this court is doing to the citizens of my community."

Her words were riveting, especially as she spoke of living in fear while being under DEA surveillance. But after all the evocative descriptions of terror and suffering, she settled into a concise but powerful plea.

"I respectfully decline to ever participate in anything that hurts my community," Goldsberry concluded. "I beg you not to make me do that."

By the time she stepped down from the witness stand, she had moved a good number of courtroom spectators to tears.

Recalcitrant Witness James Blair

James Blair was the next witness called to testify, and he presented as an affable hippie with a fluffy beard and blond hair growing towards his shoulders. Though he had also taken on the alias "James Squatter" or "Jim Squatter," he was sworn in under the surname Blair for these proceedings.

During his oath, as it's traditionally given, Blair was asked to tell the truth, the whole truth, and nothing but the truth. His enthusiastic response of, "If you'll allow it, yes!" showed the spirit of his approach.

When prosecutor Bevan asked the witness if he had been served the subpoena, Blair mentioned a change of date on the document and said that he had only received it the day before. Blair did recall receiving some order that indicated immunity, but was unsure of its significance. "Since no one was representing me, I didn't know if it was valid," he said simply.

Bevan then explained the concept of immunity and assured Blair that this order applied to any testimony he might give in this case. "Do you understand what I'm saying?" the prosecutor asked.

"That you're trying to act as my attorney," Blair shot back with a winning smile.

The comment prompted the judge to jump in and make another explanation of immunity, finally eliciting Blair's verbal agreement that he understood the situation. This established, Bevan proceeded with a question about whether Blair had received marijuana from the defendant in this case.

"At this time, I guess I'm defying the court order," Blair said casually, backing up his defiance with a declaration that he would refuse to answer all further questions.

A reminder of the immunity offer and of the penalties for contempt did nothing to dissuade him. When Blair stepped down from the stand, the official count of recalcitrant witnesses went up by one.

Recalcitrant Witness Cory Okie

The last of the witnesses to state his intentions was a young man named Cory Okie, who had traveled all the way from his new home in Oregon in order to make the hearing. He had brought his attorney along with him, and she did her best to argue that the immunity orders did not contain factual statements about her client's involvement.

"This is the first person who says they don't know anything about it at all,'" the judge said of Okie's claims. "If there's a factual dispute, what can I do? You may be right, I don't know. We'll call the witness and see what he says."

But, like his peers, Okie wasn't talking.

He remained silent even when faced with a reading of the testimony the prosecutor had intended him to give, which detailed a marijuana purchase from Rosenthal all the way down to the strain types: Max-49 and Romulan. In the end, though, all the rhetoric was just a futile exercise. Once the details of the immunity offer had been cleared up, the witness had one thing, and one thing only, to say on the stand, "With all due respect to the court, I refuse to answer that question."

And with those words, the group of witnesses was unanimous in its refusal.

Consequences

Positions and intentions fully demonstrated, the question of punishment was now heavy on the minds of all parties. Judge Breyer turned first to the prosecutor for feedback on this issue, saying, "Assuming I find these people in contempt, what is the government's position on what sanctions are appropriate?"

There was no indecision or hesitation in Bevan's presentation as he summarized the government's proposal. He requested the witnesses be found in civil contempt, and an inquiry made to determine whether incarceration would convince any of them to testify.

Agreeing readily to this course of action, Judge Breyer called all of the recalcitrant witnesses and their attorneys to come stand in front of his bench.

He had barely begun making the inquiry when he was interrupted with an argument. Brian Lundeen's attorney stepped up to say that Tuesday morning would be the first opportunity the witnesses would have to *actually* refuse to testify, and so they ought not to be held in contempt until then.

Judge Breyer was noticeably perturbed, but dispatched the matter quickly. "I find Mr. Lundeen in contempt now," he declared. As for the other witnesses, they could immediately be found in contempt as well, if they should choose to take the same stance.

The crowd quieted at these words, and Judge Breyer continued with his determination. He turned to the line of witnesses stretched before him. "Anyone who believes three days in jail would change his mind, step forward."

Blair took a conspicuous step backwards, to the delight of many in the spectator seats.

Judge Breyer deferred once again to the prosecutor, asking him what should be done. As usual, Bevan gave clear direction without delay. The prosecutor suggested finding the witnesses to be in contempt, then ordering them back on a day when the jury would be present, thereby giving them one last opportunity to change their minds and testify. The judge took Bevan's advice to the letter and ordered the witnesses back at 8am on Tuesday, May 29th.

"I am not imposing any sanctions on you now," Judge Breyer told the witnesses. "You can purge your contempt if you change your mind and testify."

Roughly a dozen U.S. Marshals had gathered in the courtroom to await the decision on whether or not to incarcerate, but they soon realized they would be leaving empty-handed and gradually exited the courtroom without fulfillment.

But Breyer had a few more words to offer about the freedom of the witnesses. Although they were being found in contempt, he assured them that it was civil contempt. However, he noted, this designation would not preclude the prosecutor from turning civil contempt into its own criminal proceeding if he decided to separately indict the recalcitrant witnesses for their refusal to testify.

All these threats were plainly incongruent, given that the defendant himself wasn't facing incarceration. During pre-trial hearings, Bevan had repeatedly assured the court that he would not seek a sentence beyond the one-day jail term that Rosenthal had already served. The recalcitrant witnesses, however, were facing at least three times that sentence.

It was an oddity of justice that was also noted by Judge Breyer. "The irony does not escape me," the judge said with emphasis, "that the witness would spend a longer time in custody than the defendant would if convicted." As for remedy, however, he offered none.

Judge Breyer did, however, offer words of commendation and praise.

In his eyes, the witnesses' behavior during the hearing proved "that you can express your views in a civilized and appropriate way that actually adds dignity to the views that you express." To the judge, this was a shining example of proper courtroom behavior.

"These are sensitive issues which are held very strongly," Judge Breyer told the witnesses before they departed, "but I will say the decorum today was excellent."

Business As Usual

As warm words escorted the witnesses from the courtroom, the judge and counsel got down to business. With closing arguments nearly upon them, and deliberation sure to follow, the jury instructions had to be ready to go. Most elements of the document were straightforward and easily agreed upon, except when it came to the sticky issues of the case.

Bevan was quick to note that witness testimony had made

Photo 33 - Robert Amparán
by Vanessa Nelson

many references to medical marijuana during the trial, and he requested the judge instruct the jury not to consider this issue at all. Judge Breyer said that it would have been too difficult to cut the witnesses off every time they said something about patients, and these mentions were of little consequence in his view. "I have the last word in this case," the judge assured Bevan, "so I can instruct the jury as need be."

Judge Breyer also ordered the defense to make no mention of jury nullification in its closing statements. "I hope it doesn't come up," he said with a tinge of nervousness.

Moving on, the judge summarily dismissed the defense's additions to the list of jury instructions. "I've looked at further instructions submitted by the defense," Judge Breyer noted, "and I'm not inclined to grant any of them."

But there was one proposal the defense hadn't mentioned yet: that Rosenthal wanted to speak during the closing statements.

"I said that it was strange, but that I'd ask the court," said defense attorney Robert Amparán while presenting the request to Judge Breyer. The judge, however, wouldn't even entertain the idea, and ruled that the defendant could not participate in his own closing argument.

Rosenthal, who was wearing sunglasses due to an eye injury, was outraged by the judge's flat denial. He saw the refusal as yet another attempt to stifle his speech, and he would not let it pass by without commentary. "I can't speak for myself during my own close?!" Rosenthal demanded, incensed. "I want that on record too, so the whole world can hear it!"

Photo 34 - Ed Rosenthal wearing dark glasses by Vanessa Nelson

Judge Breyer reminded the defendant that there was still a chance for him to testify, if he really wanted to be heard in front of a jury. That offer, however, only increased Rosenthal's displeasure. "I can only testify if I can have my corroborating witnesses, and since I can't have my corroborating witnesses, you are not allowing me to testify, in effect," Rosenthal explained, going around the logic of it once more.

"Why didn't you do that to the government and say, 'you can't have this guy, you can't have that guy, you can't have that guy,' and then they have no case?" the defendant asked.

But Rosenthal made his speeches only to the air. Surely some were listening, but there was no response. Instead, the defendant was simply reminded that he would be ordered to remain in the building during deliberations, and the court then adjourned for the long weekend.

It left a strange impression, to see the juxtaposition here. The afternoon had begun by addressing witnesses who were devoted to remaining silent, and for whose testimony the government and the court expended substantial amounts of energy. Contrasted to this was the defendant, who was passionate about talking to the world on the subject of his case, and whose speeches and outbursts the court was taking pains to overlook. The speech of the witnesses was intensively sought, while the defendant continually charged the court with disregarding his.

In both cases, speech is equally important. Be it through the silence of the uncooperative witnesses or through Rosenthal's bombast and loquacity, these ways are all a defense, and they all demonstrate bravery in the face of mighty challenges. It's a profound meditation on the strength of personal beliefs, and on the risks and sacrifices that are necessary to defend those beliefs.

The uncooperative witnesses in the Rosenthal re-trial should be regarded as nothing short of political heroes. As throughout much of modern history, it is to such courageous individuals that we owe the expansion of our civil rights and individual freedoms. And it is only through devotion in totality, as these extraordinary men and women have demonstrated, that some measure of justice can prevail.

U.S. vs. Ed Rosenthal 2.0

Tuesday, May 29th, 2007
Closing Arguments & Deliberation

Closing arguments in the re-trial of Ed Rosenthal followed a pattern that had become quite familiar. The government established a slow, methodical tedium during the early stages of the trial, and prosecutor Bevan maintained it to the very end. The defense, on the other hand, employed an escalation of outrageous language that eventually earned reprimand.

It was nothing out of the ordinary when compared to the rest of the trial, but spectators nevertheless packed the courtroom beyond capacity. The audience squeezed together on the unyielding wooden pews, while wheelchairs jammed the aisle-ways and late arrivals lined the wall.

One Last Witness

The day began early, when the last recalcitrant witness entered the courtroom at 8am. Kathleen Cappetti had been absent for Friday's show of solidarity against the government, but today she single-handedly carried the spirit of resistance through to the final week of the trial. After being sworn in, she read aloud a statement explaining her refusal to testify. "I must be compelled to answer to a higher authority," she said in a tone that was at once delicate and obstinate.

With careful composure, Cappetti listened as the prosecutor detailed an accusation that she purchased marijuana from the defendant for distribution at The Hemp Center. Then she declared she was falling back on her 5th Amendment right, claiming that the government's offer of immunity was not sufficient to protect her from self-incrimination. Under the current offer, Cappetti explained, her testimony could not be used as evidence against her, but she could still be prosecuted on matters that she testified about.

After hearing this, the prosecutor made a request that Cappetti be found in civil contempt. She was declared as such, and therefore added one more voice to the official resistance in this case.

After excusing Capetti from the stand, Judge Breyer called all of the recalcitrant witnesses to stand collectively before him. "Do any individuals wish to purge their contempt and testify?" he asked.

The only return was total silence, and it delivered its message with powerful clarity. "Okay," the judge said to the group, "you are excused." His words inspired smiles of pride, relief and validation as the witnesses left the courtroom.

The Government Closes

This last matter resolved, the government could finally rest its case and move on to closing arguments. The momentum of the proceedings began to slow down considerably at this time, as prosecutor Bevan undertook a thorough and unrelentingly dull review of the evidence. One by one, and count by count, he wrote down all the components of evidence that he saw as proving the case against Rosenthal.

The testimony of cooperative witnesses weighed heavily in this account of proof, but Bevan also wove in many inferences about phone logs, orders of growing supplies, and records of electricity usage. The prosecutor had such an abundance of this evidence in connection with the Mandela Parkway and E. 22nd Street locations that his presentation soon grew tiresome. Jurors yawned through the droning talk of money orders and bank statements, and by the end of the argument the judge looked practically comatose.

In spite of the tedium, there was nonetheless the occasional surprise in the government's argument. For the first time, Bevan presented a detailed theory about the purpose of the 67 baggies of marijuana that were found in the defendant's glove compartment. Although he initially described them as pre-weighed and pre-packaged for sale, the prosecutor now said the baggies were not intended for Rosenthal to sell on the street. Rather, Bevan argued, these were sampler packets of the various strains of marijuana that Rosenthal produced. Struck by the novelty of the government's new theory, the audience members sat up a little higher in their chairs and appeared temporarily more alert.

As Bevan's presentation wore on, however, it became apparent that the prosecutor was least confident about the showing he had made regarding the Harm Reduction Center. The law enforcement officers who testified for the prosecution were the witnesses Bevan had held up as most credible, but they had failed to establish a link between the defendant and the grow operation at that site.

DEA surveillance noted a short visit Rosenthal made to HRC while carrying a grocery bag of unknown contents, but this was hardly enough to prove any involvement in cultivation at that facility. The government was instead relying on testimony from Bob Martin and James Halloran, who merely testified that Rosenthal had spoken about getting involved with a grow operation at the HRC. It was a lackluster demonstration of culpability, especially without the more substantial testimony the prosecutor had expected from Rick Watts.

Regarding that disappointment, Bevan said about Watts to the jury, "I'll tell you candidly: he did not have a good day on the witness stand. I don't know what he had for breakfast, or for lunch, but he left his memory at home."

Attributing the lack of recall to a poor choice of breakfast foods made little sense, and Bevan's claims about the activities at the Harm Reduction Center began to look flimsier and flimsier as he lined them all up in a row. That is, until he finally mentioned one that could actually stick -- the checks that had been written to Rosenthal by Bob Martin of the HRC.

Since Martin's attempt to stop payment on those checks had escalated into a small claims suit between him and Rosenthal in 2004, there was a record of these documents above and beyond witness testimony. At least one check had carried a memo "For Consulting Fees," and if the jury could be convinced that the referenced consultations had to do with setting up a marijuana grow operation, the conspiracy charges could appear to have a more solid foundation. Alternately, if the jury could be convinced that the memo notation was merely a cover for plant sales between Rosenthal and HRC, all the better for the prosecution's case.

After profusely thanking the jurors for their service, Bevan expressed his confidence that the "clear and overwhelming" evidence had adequately proven Rosenthal's guilt. In conclusion, he simply asked the jury to hold the defendant accountable for what he had done.

The Defense Closes

As had become typical during the trial, the defense team was left to provide the spice and the zeal...and it did not disappoint. If the jurors had gotten hungry for a colorful metaphor or analogy, lead attorney Robert Amparán had handfuls of them to offer. After guiding his monologue through several objections and multiple dimensions of imagery, Amparán eventually told the jury that there was no Santa Claus. He also likened the federal government to an ostrich with its head in the sand, ignoring science and medicine. And, finally, he compared Rosenthal's situation to that of a child whose mother and father give commands that conflict with one another, suggesting that the defendant will be punished no matter which set of rules he follows.

But Amparán's imagery was not merely for entertainment value.

Photo 35 - Robert Amparán talking to reporters by Vanessa Nelson

It was a necessary vehicle for expressing important concepts about which direct expression had been thwarted. In fact, Amparán began his closing argument with straightforward language, and didn't abandon it until repeated admonitions forced him into a rhetorical corner.

"I love my country," the defense told the jury at the start of his speech. "I love my state. But I fear my government."

Bevan immediately objected, calling the statements improper. Even after Judge Breyer sustained the objection and advised counsel not to testify to the jury, Amparán nonetheless continued, clarifying that he fears his government because it lies misleads and distorts the truth. He began to speak of his own experience as a Mexican-American who was just "one generation out of the fields," but the judge and prosecutor protested more fiercely this time and cut the defense attorney off.

Amparán regrouped and started constructing a comparison to the Scopes Monkey Trial, characterizing it as a case in which a federal restriction prevented a teacher from presenting scientific evidence of human evolution. Bevan objected at this point, and Judge Breyer echoed the prosecutor's recollection that the Scopes case was not federal. The judge instructed the jury that there was no evidence to support Amparán's half-assembled analogy.

Shortly following this, Amparán simply grabbed the ball and made a run for it. "The court and the government have told you that state law doesn't apply, that there's no medical marijuana in federal court," the defense attorney recounted to the jury. "But when someone has cancer, when someone is dying of AIDS—"

Judge Breyer tackled him before he could score, and ordered the jury to disregard the comments. "You know this is improper!" he said, shaming Amparán,

No amount of scolding could dissuade the defense from making a second attempt, and shortly thereafter, Amparán had started in again. "The federal government has deemed marijuana illegal," he began. "The federal government has deemed marijuana to have no medical benefits."

When Judge Breyer cut in to forbid arguments about scheduling and statements about the medical aspects of marijuana, Amparán tried a reverse tactic. "Let me contrast that with what the federal government has said *does* have medical benefit," he proposed.

Judge Breyer immediately declared the topic inappropriate.

Sufficiently warmed up, Amparán went in for his showstopper. He turned to the jury and said that there have been times in history when the federal government has done things that it later admitted were not the right things to do. He then began listing some of these subjects, "Civil rights, slavery, deportation of U.S. citizens of Mexican descent during the Depression, internment of Japanese during World War II—"

But Judge Breyer wouldn't allow the jurors to hear another word of it. He immediately sent them out of the room and began questioning Amparán about the motive behind his argument.

"The analogies of Japanese internment, slavery, civil rights," the judge said, listing off the defense attorney's examples. "I don't see why it's proper to argue that unless what you're seeking is nullification by the jury."

Amparán explained that he was merely trying to demonstrate that the government makes mistakes and sometimes makes bad laws, but the judge was only further dismayed by this clarification. "It's not about whether the law is just or unjust," Judge Breyer said about the jury's consideration. "It's about whether the witnesses are telling the truth."

"That's not my argument," Amparán countered. He quickly moved forward to tell the judge that there were many more controversial subjects he planned to address during his closing argument: the war in Iraq, Osama Bin Laden, weapons of mass destruction, the failure of the federal government to adequately deal with the consequences of Hurricane Katrina...

He had barely penetrated his list before he was overcome by thunderous applause from the packed spectator seats.

The cheering crowd caused Judge Breyer to hit the roof. "I'll clear the courtroom if there's another outburst like that!" he warned the audience sternly. On that note, he turned to the defense attorney and ordered him to avoid speaking about any of the aforementioned subjects during his closing statements.

When the jurors re-entered the courtroom, Amparán engaged them to think more abstractly and symbolically. He began to expand on a metaphor he had created earlier in his argument, and ended up giving enough talk about rotten fish to ruin a few appetites.

The defense attorney suggested that the charges in the case are like a recipe. Each charge has certain elements, just as each recipe has certain ingredients. To get a good result, the right elements must be put in at the correct time and in the correct way. As Amparán argued, the federal government possessed the ingredients in this case for so long that they eventually spoiled, and just a single spoiled ingredient can taint the whole stew.

"If it smells rotten, like it would make you sick, you have the right to reject it," he told the jury passionately.

Bordering on belaboring the analogy, Amparán clarified that the rotten fish in this case were the government witnesses. He ran through a quick character assassination, attacking their motivations and their credibility. "These are people you wouldn't want to have a cup of coffee with or buy a used car from," the defense attorney concluded for the jurors. "You don't trust them, and so you wouldn't want to base a guilty verdict on that trust. "

And Amparán cautioned that the verdict must be one that the jurors can stand behind on a continuing basis. After all, he reminded them, "At the end of the day, you step back into the land of California."

Winding to a close, Amparán spoke a great deal about his faith in the jurors and their ultimate decision. True, he admitted, there were certain topics he couldn't bring up during the trial, and certain questions he couldn't ask. Still, he expressed full confidence that the jurors had sufficient knowledge, understanding, courage, compassion, life experience, and common sense to do the right thing.

Throughout his speech, he had reinforced the notion of independence and safety. "No one can force you to disclose the reasons for your verdict," Amparán said, reiterating the concept a final time in parting. "You cannot be punished for your verdict. You are protected. You are safe."

The Government's Rebuttal

Bevan was then given an opportunity to briefly respond to the defense's closing arguments.

He directed notice to the fact that the defense didn't attack the substance of witness testimony, nor did they mention the various boxes of evidence. He wondered if they simply had no explanation when confronted with the physical evidence, and if they conceded the 33,000 plants found at Rosenthal's properties.

That last mention nearly slipped by, but Amparán objected to the plant count, indignant. Bevan then had to go back and correct himself, "I mean 3,000 plants."

But the main function of his rebuttal was to make the final plea in the ears of the jury. "Other than to stick a label on a witness as a liar or a drug addict," the prosecutor urged, "I ask you to evaluate the physical evidence. Consider what evidence has been addressed and what has not been addressed. Base your decision on the evidence. Base your decision on the law as Judge Breyer will instruct you."

Deliberations

And instruct he certainly did, although there were no surprises in Judge Breyer's final orders to the jury. He reviewed the charges, as well as the specific elements that would need to be proven in order to arrive at a guilty verdict. The judge also clarified which pieces of information should be considered as evidence and which should not, and defined different types of evidence.

The job of the jury, Judge Breyer reinforced, was simply to decide if the defendant was guilty or not guilty of the charges. Sentencing, he warned, would be an entirely separate matter. It would not be determined by the jury, nor ought it to be considered by the jury.

The jurors retired for deliberations after a late lunch, but by the end of the afternoon the courtroom was abuzz once again – the jury had sent in a question for the judge. All parties fell into their proper place, eager to address the inquiry.

As expected, the jurors were having some difficulty determining the requirements of the conspiracy charges, and were particularly unsure about the conspiracy charge regarding the Harm Reduction Center.

Essentially, the question asked: if Rosenthal knew that the marijuana he distributed to the HRC would ultimately be distributed to patients, then does that make Rosenthal a co-conspirator with the HRC on the charges?

After some reflection and a little bit of research, counsel crafted some proposals for their answer. Though restricted from making any determination for the jury, the attorneys and the judge nevertheless hammered out an agreement on the generalities of what must be shown to prove the charges.

"The mere existence of a buyer/seller relationship does not prove a conspiracy to distribute marijuana," Judge Breyer concluded. For conspiracy, it would be necessary to establish that the seller was part of a further agreement to distribute the product beyond the original, intended buyer.

There was some wrangling over what word should be used to describe the object that was being distributed. As the clock neared 5pm, the judge finally settled on the term "controlled substance" and arranged for the answer to be provided to the jurors when they reconvened on Wednesday, May 30th, at 8:30am.

The defense attorneys were displeased by the nature and the subject of the jury question. "It looks like they're going to convict on the charges for Mandela Parkway," Amparán said to courtroom observers.

As for the charges regarding the Harm Reduction Center, Amparán had the sense that the jurors were attempting to make the charges fit the defendant. "They're trying to connect the dots for the government, rather than tossing this," he said bleakly.

Wednesday, May 30th, 2007
The Verdicts

As the jury began its second day of deliberations, Rosenthal was in good spirits. "The longer they're out, the more optimistic I become," he said with a serene smile, standing amongst the supporters who milled about the courtroom doorway and lounged apprehensively in the hallway.

And out they were…at least until lunchtime drew nigh. It was then that there was clamor in the court, with hushed expectant voices whispering, "There's been a note!"

But what felt like resolution was actually far from it. On his bench, Judge Breyer puzzled over the piece of paper, patting his fingertips on his mouth in contemplation for a few moments. Then, he explained: the jurors could not agree on one of the counts, and were asking for advice on how to proceed. A flurry of speculation followed, bouncing between the judge and the attorneys.

Prosecutor Bevan began, "If they can't agree on one count, but agree on the others--"

Judge Breyer interjected, saying it was merely assumption that verdicts had been reached on the other four counts. Certainly the note implied this, but didn't actually state it outright. Nonetheless, he was perfectly happy to engage in exercises of the hypothetical. "If, in fact, four verdicts have been reached…the government could dismiss the unresolved count and we could take the other four verdicts," the judge said, proposing what appeared to be the path of least resistance.

But Bevan simply shrugged away the possibility, inspiring the judge to reinforce the proposal. "You're not going to re-try this case, right?" the judge frowned down at the prosecutor. "So, what's the point? It's gone on long enough. I don't see the point."

For clarification, Judge Breyer quickly composed and dispatched a note to the jury, asking, "Have you reached verdicts as to the other four counts?"

This process of passing notes, with so much analysis and strategizing following each exchange, created an atmosphere of metaphysical suspense. Carefully phrased questions, which were promptly returned with disembodied but weighty answers, had all the trappings of prophecy and divination. And, like magic, the judge's note was quickly returned from the secret back room, marked 'yes.'

There was some muted babble amongst the audience, no doubt whispering predictions about the nature of those verdicts. It continued as Judge Breyer summoned the jurors and the courtroom waited for their emergence. A few observers used the pause in activity to duck out into the hallway and call waiting friends or press contacts.

Anticipation was acute as the jurors filed in, their somber faces belying the rigors of deliberation. The judge asked for the foreman and discovered it was the man who was seated closest to him – Mr. Bobby Bynum of El Cerrito. The former naval machinist sat with his hands folded and answered the questions posed by the judge.

"Is the jury hopelessly deadlocked?" Judge Breyer addressed the foreman, who commanded all the eyes in the courtroom.

"Yes," Bynum answered plainly.

The judge then posed the opposite question, asking if there was a reasonable probability they would come to a unanimous decision if given more time in the jury room. He received a reply in the affirmative, which was so unexpected that he had to ask twice to confirm it.

Given the stated possibility of resolution, the judge concluded there was no choice but to send the jurors back to deliberate further. After they had left the room, Judge Breyer rolled his eyes and quipped, "This is why I'm out of the business of prediction."

The scenery relapsed back into its previous posture of anxious expectance. Soon afterwards, however, it became clear that Judge Breyer was eager to push the process forward. Those who waited inside witnessed him emerge from his back chambers and storm to the front of the courtroom shortly before 1pm, calling for the prosecutor. What followed was a pressured plea for Bevan to relent and drop the unresolved charge.

"I strongly urge you to go talk to the office," Judge Breyer directed the prosecutor, referring to the office of the U.S. Attorney on the courthouse's 10th floor.

Persisting at this point, the judge argued, would be a waste of time. If the jury had already reached four guilty verdicts, then what was the use of one more? And if the jury had decided to acquit on four of the counts, would the prosecutor really proceed to try the 5th count again? "You're not going to do that in front of *me*," Judge Breyer told Bevan firmly.

The prosecutor plodded off to the elevators quietly, returning not only with his orders but also with the issuer of those orders – Scott Schools, U.S. Attorney for the Northern District of California. A surprise guest, Schools squeezed inconspicuously into the third row of courtroom seats to watch the verdicts come down.

Approaching the bench, Bevan told the judge that the U.S. Attorney would dismiss the unresolved count only if it was Count 1, the charge that alleged Rosenthal had conspired with Ken Hayes and Rick Watts to manufacture or distribute marijuana at San Francisco's Harm Reduction Center. This announcement prompted another round of note passing between the judge and the jury room, which revealed that the count in question was indeed Count 1.

This was the magical answer, and the judge immediately sent for the jury to give the remaining four verdicts. It was a sudden turn of events that propelled spectators into a heated hurry. After the false alarm they had received earlier, courtroom observers had expected a couple more hours of tedious anticipation. Now, they scrambled to quickly reassemble supporters and reporters alike. It was a tall order. Many failed to arrive in time to hear the verdicts firsthand, leading to intensive questioning sessions in the hallway once court adjourned.

When the solemn jury assembled again in the courtroom, this time it was for real. The verdict sheet passed from the foreman to the judge, who gave it a quick scan before handing it over to the court clerk for announcement. The woman that spectators had come to know merely as "Barbara" was a good pick as the agent for publicly delivering the verdicts. A sweet-faced woman with an accommodating nature and thick gray hair down to her hips, she was the kind of person who could deliver bad news without inspiring spite or resentment. As such, she began her recitation.

Barbara reiterated that there had been no verdict on Count 1, identifying it once again as the conspiracy charge relating to cultivation at the Harm Reduction Center. Bevan was quick to clarify that the government would drop this count only against Rosenthal, thereby retaining the right to prosecute the other two parties named in the charge: Ken Hayes and Rick Watts. Though subtly put, the revelation only reinforced recently circulated rumors that Watts had been taken into the custody of federal agents the previous weekend.

Moving along, Barbara read a not guilty verdict as to Count 2, which was the substantive charge for the use of the Harm Reduction Center to knowingly cultivate marijuana. Logic seemed to fall into place with the verdict on this charge – since the jury couldn't decide whether the defendant had planned to do it or not, it only made good sense that they would find that there was no proof that he had actually done it.

The guilty verdicts began streaming in, however, as soon as there was a change in the scene of the crimes. The jury found Rosenthal guilty on Count 4, which charged him with cultivating and distributing marijuana, as well as possessing marijuana with the intent to distribute, at his Oakland property. Through Count 5, Rosenthal was found guilty of using this Oakland property to manufacture and distribute marijuana. And, finally, the jurors reached a guilty verdict on Count 3, which was the conspiracy charge related to all the crimes detailed in Counts 4 and 5.

When it came to charges related to San Francisco, Rosenthal was exonerated. For activities that occurred in Oakland, however, he was once again convicted. It seemed an odd twist that all of the guilty verdicts pertained to cultivation in Oakland, where Rosenthal had been deputized by the city to provide medical cannabis. But, considering that the jury was not permitted to hear any evidence that Rosenthal had been deputized, the result was really not so surprising. In fact, it was all too predictable.

Courtroom spectators did not anticipate the prosecutor's next remarks, however. Following the reading of the verdicts, Bevan sent the audience into audible outrage by bringing up the issue of bail status and reminding the judge that Rosenthal had just been convicted on charges that required remand into custody. As the crowd grumbled, the prosecutor continued by stating that he would recommend that Rosenthal remain on the same bail status. Satisfied that no one would be dragged to jail that afternoon, the audience nonetheless held onto its suspicion for the remainder of the proceedings.

All that was left, however, were some pleasantries and farewells. Judge Breyer thanked the jury for their service, saying,

"You have been an extraordinarily conscientious jury," and arranged to meet them in the jury room later for further expressions of gratitude.

This author was fortunate enough to have the opportunity to speak to one of the jurors in a courthouse elevator, following the announcement of the verdict. When questioned about whether evidence of Rosenthal's deputization would have made a difference in the consideration of the charges, Jon Noda required further explanation on the facts. He was given a quick summary of the situation, after which he was reflective. "Maybe," said the middle-aged quality engineer from Fremont. "It depends. I'd have to know more."

The response, though simplistic, cut straight to the essence of the defense's complaint – deprived of information, the jury would be incapable of arriving at a just and moral decision. And each of Rosenthal's attorneys had a similar perspective when questioned about the situation.

Robert Amparán spent his first few sentences eulogizing. "This is a sad day for justice. This is a sad day for patients." He then

Photo 36 - Shari Greenberger
"Justice has not been served."
by Vanessa Nelson

remarked snidely, "It's pretty frightening when you see the federal government scrambling to hide the truth."

About the fact that Rosenthal had been deputized, Amparán continued, "It was not part of the jury's world of evidence, so I think there was some concern about whether this was within the realm of state law." He then conceded, "I understand what the jury did. They did basically what the judge told them to do."

Defense attorney Shari Greenberger put the matter in absolute terms. "Justice has not been served," she declared passionately. "The jury has been deceived. And we will do everything in our power to make sure the whole truth comes out."

In the meantime, Greenberger urged Rosenthal's supporters to be inspired rather than downtrodden. "I want to encourage everyone to not feel discouraged by this outcome but to feel empowered," she said exuberantly.

Omar Figueroa of the defense team compared the situation to one faced by Americans in the early part of the 20th Century. "Prohibition of alcohol ended when jurors started refusing to convict people accused under an unfair law," he reminded a small crowd of reporters and advocates. "I am telling all future and potential jurors that you have the power to nullify."

Photo 37 - Omar Figueroa "I am telling all future and potential jurors that you have the power to nullify" by Vanessa Nelson

Rosenthal himself was characteristically dramatic after the verdict, saying of the jurors, "When they get all the information, they will regret for the rest of their lives that they were called upon by the federal government to make an immoral decision."

Rosenthal promptly filed a motion for a new trial, continuing the legal process. Whether in Breyer's courtroom or another, the case will surely be heard again in some form. Indeed, it was tried this time around with one eye on the proceedings in district court and one eye in foresight of the review by an appellate court.

"It's a long way from being over," Amparán said immediately after hearing the verdicts, assuring the public that the momentum of the Rosenthal case is as fast and strong as ever.

Rosenthal maintained his high spirits and joked merrily to the supporters who encircled him outside the federal courthouse. With a characteristic grin, he made the prediction, "We'll all be smoking joints here in a few years."

Photo 38 - Ed Rosenthal "We'll all be smoking joints here in a few years"
by Vanessa Nelson

The Verdicts

U.S. vs. Ed Rosenthal 2.0

About the Author

Vanessa Nelson's accomplishments have been shaped by two lifelong drives: dedication to activism and a passion for writing. During her early youth, Vanessa was heavily involved in community service organizations and also volunteered long hours tutoring struggling students in a variety  of academic subjects. At the same time, she was developing a strong writing voice that won countless essay contest prizes and opened the door to higher education. For college, Vanessa chose an institution famous for its history of activism -- the University of California at Berkeley. At the turn of the millennium, she graduated ahead of her class and received her bachelor's degree in Mass Communications. Expanding her skills from one medium to another, Vanessa was employed writing copy for a travel publication and also spent three years composing news broadcasts for an FM radio station. It was not until getting involved in the medical marijuana movement, however, that Vanessa discovered a successful way to make use of her writing ability while also serving her interests as an activist. Quickly finding her niche in reporting on the court cases of medical marijuana defendants in California, Vanessa has emerged as a premiere new talent in this field. Her engaging style, her keen eye for accuracy and her aggressive pursuit of a story all combine to make her one of the most promising young writers of the new generation.

Printed in Great Britain
by Amazon

83083545R00089